My Father
Bertrand Russell

MY FATHER
BERTRAND RUSSELL

by

KATHARINE TAIT

LONDON
VICTOR GOLLANCZ LTD
1976

ISBN 0 575 02111 X

92
R961t

Printed in Great Britain by
Lowe & Brydone (Printers) Ltd., Thetford, Norfolk

To the memory of my father
And the future of my children
This book is affectionately dedicated
By the link between them.

—Katharine Tait

Contents

People in My Father's Life

Grandmother Russell
> Lady Frances Anna Maria Elliot, second wife of Lord John Russell

Lord John Russell
> Son of the sixth Duke of Bedford, prime minister of England, first Earl Russell

Amberley
> John Russell, Viscount Amberley, son of Lord John and Lady Frances, father of Bertrand Russell

Kate Stanley
> Daughter of Lord Stanley of Alderley, wife of Amberley, mother of Bertrand Russell

Uncle Frank
> Francis Russell, second Earl Russell, older brother of Bertrand Russell

My father
> Bertrand Arthur William Russell, F.R.S., O.M., third Earl Russell

Alys
> Alys Pearsall-Smith, sister of Logan Pearsall-Smith, Bertrand Russell's first wife

Ottoline
> Lady Ottoline Morrell, wife of Philip Morrell

Colette

> Lady Constance Malleson, wife of actor Miles Malleson, actress under the stage name of Colette O'Niel

Dora

> Dora Winifred Black, Bertrand Russell's second wife, my mother

Peter

> Patricia Helen Spence, Bertrand Russell's third wife, Conrad's mother

Edith

> Edith Bronson Finch, Bertrand Russell's fourth wife

John

> John Conrad Russell, fourth Earl Russell, Bertrand Russell's eldest son, born November 1921

Conrad

> Conrad Russell, Bertrand Russell's second son, born April 1937

Kate

> Katharine Jane Russell, Bertrand Russell's daughter, born December 1923

Harriet

> Harriet Barry, Dora's daughter

Roddy

> Roderick Barry, Dora's son

Susan

> Susan Lindsay, daughter of Vachel Lindsay, John's wife

Charlie

> Charles Tait, Kate's husband

John's girls

> Anne, Sarah and Lucy Russell

Kate's children

> David, Anne, Jonathan, Andrew and Benjamin Tait

Preface

What was it like, having Bertrand Russell for a father? Was he stern, remote, analytical? Did he demand absolute quiet while he wrestled with philosophical conundrums and wrote his innumerable books? Was he too lofty to concern himself with the trivial affairs of his children? What was he really like?

I have been asked such questions all my life and have struggled vainly to provide concise and honest answers. Two kinds of questions are mixed up here, and they need different kinds of answers.

"What was he like as a father?" people ask. I can answer that with description: how he looked, what he said, what he ate for breakfast, what he did when we were bad. But "What was it like having Bertrand Russell for a father?" involves much more: What was the atmosphere in our home? How did it affect us? How do I feel about it now, after so many years?

Somebody once asked me if I ever argued with my father. The question struck me as preposterous, for of course it was quite impossible. His mind was as sharp as a razor and as quick as a steel trap, and his fund of knowledge was apparently infinite. I have never seen or heard anybody get the better of him in an argument.

He used to tell us often and gleefully the tale of Socrates and the Sophist (or was it the Sophist and the foolish young man?) who was a son of a bitch. It went like this:

SOCRATES: Is that your dog?

SOPHIST: Yes, it is.

SOCRATES: Is it a female?

SOPHIST: Yes, it is.

SOCRATES: Is she a mother?

SOPHIST: Yes, she is.

SOCRATES: Then she is your dog and your mother and you are a son of a bitch.

We had a dog, once, who went on walks with us and chased after rabbits, following his nose. We, who walked upright and used our eyes instead of our noses, would see a rabbit run across the path ahead of us, while Sherry, running along with his nose to the ground, saw nothing, until suddenly he came upon the delicious scent of rabbit in his path. Being a dog bred more for looks than intelligence, he often went off in the direction that the rabbit had come, rather than that in which it had gone. We watched this performance with lofty amusement, despising the poor dog for his stupidity and his inability to use his eyes as we did. But secretly I identified with the dog and felt sorry for him, the recipient of our scorn. He was not really stupid, only a dog, behaving as a dog behaves.

That is what it was like, having Bertrand Russell for a father.

My Father
Bertrand Russell

The Garden of Eden

At Platform 1 in Paddington station stands the Cornish
Riviera express, a chocolate-and-cream-colored dragon of
the great Western Railway, hissing and smoking and restless to be off. Crowds of people swarm into the station,
and among them you may glimpse the Russell family
emerging from a taxi on their annual migration to Cornwall. There is the famous philosopher himself, in a dark
suit and a grey hat, speaking to the taxi driver with the
greatest politeness. Beside him stands his young wife, ele-
gantly dressed, looking about the station with her beautiful
brown eyes, and his two small children, keeping very close
to him for protection in this bewildering place. They are
both rather untidy, more the way children look at the end
of a trip than at the beginning. Behind them is a shy governess and a small tower of luggage.

The Russells do not hurry and they do not fuss; they
know they have plenty of time, for Bertrand Russell, like
his father before him, is devoted to trains and timetables
and always knows exactly what to do at a station. He calls
a porter and tells him to put the big luggage in the van,
then meet us at the train with the small stuff. We follow
him into the echoing booking hall to buy the tickets, then

to the bookstall, where he buys himself a detective story and each child a book or a comic. After that we put pennies in the old red slot machines to buy ourselves small bars of stale chocolate. The station is full of hurrying people, honking taxis and the hooting and rumbling of heavy engines coming and going, but with my father I am not afraid. I hold his hand and gaze at the brightly lit stalls of exotic fruit and flowers, then up with the smoke and steam to the dirty glass roof high above.

When all the business is done, my father takes us down to the far end of the platform to see the engine, a very long walk, but worth it for the sight of that shining green monster. Then we walk slowly back along the train in search of an empty compartment. Finding one, we pile in and spread our coats and books over all the eight seats to make it look full. The grownups sit down and open their books, but John and I hang out of the window watching the late-comers run up and down the platform looking for empty seats. If anyone comes to our compartment, we politely move away from the door, but we make horrible idiot faces and they usually go away. My father suggested this method of discouraging fellow passengers and, unless the train was desperately crowded, it worked very well.

My father was a notably irreverent and mischievous man, not above using his children to provoke people in ways that would not be quite acceptable from conventional adults. Later, when we traveled more by car, he suggested that we might lean out of the windows when we passed other cars and shout out: "Your grandfather was a monkey!" This was to convince them of the correctness of Darwin's theory of evolution, but usually they could not hear clearly enough to get the message.

At exactly the right time, the guard blows his whistle and waves his green flag, and the train moves slowly out of the station. A connoisseur of train travel such as my father judged the skill of the engine driver by the smoothness of his start, and he would shake his head disapprovingly if we felt an unpleasant jolt.

My father's interest in trains extended to knowing every station from London to Penzance. He communicated his interest to us and felt very proud when John began to know them too. "The journey between London and Cornwall in the train," my father wrote, "interests him passionately, and he knows all the stations where the train stops or where carriages are slipped." Though I loved trains as much as John did, I always got the sequence muddled— I never knew, for instance, when we would pass the white horse, a vast picture of a horse on a hillside, made by cutting away the turf to reveal the chalk underneath. My father always knew. "We're coming to the white horse," he would say. "Look, there it is now." And there it would be, but to this day I don't know when to look to find it for myself. We passed it during lunch, I think, looking out of the wide windows of the dining car as the soup sloshed back and forth in the bowls. I imagined that he must have magic powers and could conjure up a white horse at will.

Once the train was under way, John and I explored it from end to end, while our parents sat reading and talking. We explored the train, we ate our chocolate, we read our comics and squabbled about whose turn it was to sit by the window—and still there were hours before we reached Cornwall. Then we turned to more active entertainments, such as climbing into the luggage nets above the seats, while our parents sat imperturbably and even seemed to enjoy the active energy of their young. I cannot recall ever being told to sit down and be quiet. Believing in freedom for children, they lived by their belief, even when it was not convenient. They made sure, however, that we respected their rights as much as they respected ours.

For a while in the afternoon we could amuse ourselves by looking out of the windows as the train ran along under the famous red cliffs of Devon, shrieking in and out of brief tunnels and hurrying through sandy little stations, which seemed like large toys put there for people on vacation. In those days, our own Cornish beaches were almost deserted and we looked with contempt on the poor trippers spending their short two weeks on the crowded sands of Dawlish and Teignmouth.

We were rather superior and conceited children, not for reasons of class or wealth, which would have horrified our parents, but because we thought we were wiser than others and knew better how to live. My father was a passionate believer in liberty and equality, thinking it unfair for some to be poor and others rich; but fraternity was a different matter. He was an aristocrat, who had been taught to think himself superior and to look on that superiority as an obligation to help the less fortunate. He never did believe that men are born equal in ability, and he never felt at ease with stupid, ignorant or prejudiced people, though he was quite willing to devote his life to helping them. Whereas my mother, though she gets along beautifully with working people, tends to think that those who disagree with her must be fools. And of course we thought so too, thus absorbing a double dose of pride from our devotedly democratic parents.

At long last the train pulls into Penzance station and we tumble out into the chilly seaside sunshine. But even now the journey is not over. Another ten miles, from Penzance to Porthcurno, must be covered by car or bus. Halfway between the two is the village of St. Buryan, named for one of the heroic Irish saints who came to Cornwall in sieves and thimbles to convert the heathen long ago, a landmark to us because of its unusually tall church tower.

After St. Buryan, we watch for the sea; the journey is almost over, and our restlessness fills the car. At last, over the brow of a little hill, we come to our lane and our house, the ugly castle of our dreams.

Certainly it was (and is) an ugly house, two ill-proportioned boxes stuck together, with a roof triangle on top of the larger box, and neither alteration nor imagination can make it beautiful. When my parents bought the place it was a nameless brown stucco house in the middle of a field, dark within and dull without, but they could look out of its windows to the distant ships and the sun shining on the water. My father was never happy in a house without a wide view—and here he found one to delight his heart.

On the rounded back of the farthest hill, silhouetted against the sea, were three square houses in a row, and another turned at an angle and half hidden behind the hillside. These houses my father christened Brown, Jones, & Robinson and Ebenezer Stick-in-the-Mud, and they symbolized for us respectability and oddity. Sometimes we walked past them and saw that real people lived in them, but I always regarded them as interlopers, trespassers on the property of the rightful owners.

My mother named the house "Carn Voel," after a wild headland, and she painted it white with blue and grey, to match the sea and sky and clouds. She added a wide front porch with a Chinese-looking roof, orange pillars and a floor of large slate slabs. She surrounded the house with thick hedges, to break the wind, and then she laid out a lawn and flower beds in front, vegetables and fruit behind the house. In her happiness, she wrote a poem about the house, which she called "Immortality" and put at the beginning of her book *The Right to Be Happy*. It tells how they felt about the Cornish venture and what they hoped for.

> *Blue, white, grey are the clouds*
> *And patches of grey and silver are made on the sea;*
> *And paths of blue and pearl for the ships to go.*
>
> *Blue, white, grey is the house*
> *I have made on the hilltop,*

Where the clouds shall go over and the winds shall blow
And we shall gaze on the sea,
Children and lawns and flowers shall blossom about us.

When we die
May we sleep in love;
Perhaps in the winds our thoughts will speak to our
     children.
Let people say
They were fearless in life and loved beauty,
Therefore these souls are worthy
To cleanse and ride with the majestic sea
And to speak and wander the world with the murmur-
     ing winds.

She filled the house with her energy and her laughter
and her love of bright colors. The dining room, for instance,
a cold north-facing room with only one window, she painted
with yellow walls and bright orange woodwork; then she
added curtains of yellow-and-orange Chinese silk and a
carpet the color of the night sky. It was a stimulating
background for the lively conversations around the table.
Upstairs, the bedrooms had wallpaper bright with birds and
flowers, gay curtains and a minimum of furniture. Carn
Voel was never a house for elegant living.

The house in London, by contrast, was full of beautiful
things my parents had brought home from their travels.
It provided a gracious background for their sophisticated
urban social life and served as a center for their ceaseless
activity in politics and in the service of unpopular causes.
Since we left that house when I was only three, I have
little real knowledge of my parents' London existence; but
I have seen my mother's face light up at the mere mention of 31 Sydney Street and I have heard her speak wist-
fully of the happy years she spent there.

One incident stands out: my encounter with Sidney
Webb in a dark hallway. He was not a tall man, but I was

still extremely small, and I remember him looming over me, dark suit over extended stomach, and a neatly bearded face far away above it.

"Little girl," he said, looking down at my bright eyes in the gloom, "will you give me your eyes?"—for his own were dim and gave him trouble. I burst into floods of tears, and it took my parents a long time to convince me that he did not mean it.

All my memories of the London house are dark—dark wood, dark halls, firelight on the ceiling, fog in the streets —and I much preferred the big-windowed, sunny rooms of Carn Voel, where I could have been happy all year round.

My mother and father, however, enjoyed their London life, and they valued the intellectual benefits of an urban environment for their children. We learned much simply walking in the streets and watching things, and far more from the immense wealth of museums and monuments in that great capital city. London also had nursery schools, where John could enjoy the companionship of children his own age. He went to a Montessori nursery school, which my parents considered good, I believe, though all I know of it is the tale they told about John using the Montessori apparatus to make trains instead of the proper Montessori things. According to the authorities, this showed that he had a "disordered imagination." My father, from whom John had learned his love of trains, was unimpressed.

Our family had many such treasured pomposities, punctured by ridicule and stored away for later entertainment. One of our favorites was the pronouncement of the Harley Street specialist to whom John was taken as a baby because he could not digest his food and kept on throwing up. The doctor examined him carefully, asked many questions and at last delivered himself of his solemn professional opinion:

"Ah yes, regurgitation. Four guineas, please."

London alone was not enough to prepare us for a full life. For "environment stimulates questions, and one cannot attach too much importance to varied environment in early years. I think that to create a complete modern person, we must bear in mind that two activities are of fundamental importance to our society, the practice of agriculture and the practice of industry. Every child should feel these two forces in the marrow of his bones."

"What delights the town child misses," my mother wrote, "the plunge into blue seawater, blackberrying on warm September days, watching the cows at milking, the fishermen mending their nets." Our parents wanted to be sure we would experience these pleasures, not only because they were pleasant—few things were done for that reason alone—but also because they were instructive. "A child ought to know as if by feeling it the growth of crops, the breeding of animals and human beings, the movement of tides, winds and stars, the colors and habits of flowers and trees. It ought to know also the speed and manner of mechanical activity, processes of manufacture, chemistry, dynamics."

"I feel," my mother said, speaking for both parents, "that this is what we want to produce: a creature that understands the texture and habits of its world so completely, that when exact science is added it will manipulate that world with the sureness and grace of the artist or the dancer who performs with easy abandon the most difficult of movements."

With this ambition in mind, they went looking for a house in the country, intending, like Persephone (though of their own free will), to divide their year between the dark, mechanical splendors of town and the bucolic bliss of the countryside. It was a high ambition, which was largely realized. Not that John and I turned out paragons of grace and wisdom, but we did feel we belonged to the natural world. We acquired in those early years a strong feeling for the rhythms of nature and for our part in them, which I, at least, have found a source of strength throughout my life.

Although Carn Voel was bought as a summer house for the Russell family, it was never intended for our exclusive use. There were almost always adult visitors and often extra children, some of whom stayed almost all summer. I remember four or five of us having chicken pox there together in one vacation. Plenty of people traveled to this remote big toe of Cornwall to visit the famous philosopher, or the zealous Socialist, or "dear Bertie" if they were among his many friends. John and I saw little of them and did not know who they were, though I do remember a visit from Rabindranath Tagore, a man with an impressive white beard and bare brown feet in sandals.

John and I, who went to bed very early, woke early on those bright summer mornings and lay in bed listening to the sounds of the day beginning. The coffee grinder in the kitchen; the regular strokes of the pump in the scullery, where the gardener pumped the day's water supply from the well up to the tank on the roof; the arrival of early-morning tea and shaving water for the adults. Sometimes, when the morning sun came dazzling in, we got up early and tiptoed down the stairs, out of the glass-windowed front door and into the dew-soaked garden. Even in the warmest weather, mornings were chilly and we were glad to come in to breakfast: oatmeal, without which my father's breakfast was not complete, then eggs, and finally toast, standing in cold racks on the table in the English style, to be eaten with butter and marmalade.

Visitors and family ate breakfast together, then separated, each to his own kind of morning work, to meet again at lunch. Sometimes before lunch the narrow hall outside the dining room was crowded with grown-up people who seemed, from my perspective, to be all dark legs and loud voices. More often than not the dominant voice would be my father's, for he was a great entertainer. Courtesy demanded that one entertain one's guests, and this, for him, meant keeping them laughing with an endless display of jokes and tales and dreadful puns. That narrow, crowded hall is forever associated in my mind with the summer we had a Danish governess with an unpronounceable name. Every day, memory tells me, my father would challenge the assembled company to pronounce her name, and none could do it to his satisfaction. Then, looking down, he would say: "Kate, can you say it?"

Hot and embarrassed, I would close up my throat and choke out: "Högström" (or whatever it was).

"There you are," he would say, with his startling laugh. "She says it better than any of you!"

I was proud, of course, but not quite happy. I felt more comfortable silently lost among the legs, like a dog.

At lunchtime John and I sat at a low small table of our own, where we could hear the adult conversation without disturbing it, and eat in our own messy way without offending anyone. Conversation at the adult table was always fluent and lively, and of course they all talked, but I remember only my father, carving at the head of the table, making sure everyone had enough, and generously giving out his priceless wit together with his food.

He became serious only when we had fish. Cornwall is a fishing community, and we often had fresh mackerel, gleaming and beautiful with silver and green-blue stripes, but full of tiny bones. Then he would take his spectacle case from his breast pocket, put on his spectacles and study the fish with the greatest solemnity. My heart always sank, thinking there must be something wrong with the fish. But it was merely that he couldn't see the bones without his glasses.

At the end of the afternoon, when we came back from

whatever beach we had visited, John and I had nursery tea, quickly followed by bath and bed, while the adults had afternoon tea, followed much later by grown-up dinner. Occasionally, when we were not tired enough to fall asleep instantly, we would get out of bed during grown-up dinner and creep about the house, gradually increasing our noise until it penetrated the closed dining-room door and someone came out to tell us to go back to bed. Usually the first time it would be the current governess, then my father speaking kindly and then, if we were brash enough to venture out a third time, my father looking very stern. After that, there was no more coming out.

We did not live at all grandly in Cornwall, yet I remember a cook, a housemaid, a gardener, a man to drive the car and a nanny or governess for us children. Women in my mother's position did not do their own housework in those days, even when they knew how: my mother never cared too much about such matters. As long as life went on reasonably smoothly, she occupied her mind with things genuinely more interesting than the price of vegetables or the whiteness of the wash. She believed that household concerns were as much the province of men as of women and that her sex alone was not sufficient reason to load all domestic chores on her. One year, indeed, when she was writing a book in Cornwall, she went so far as to rent a hut on the cliffs, a mile from home, in order to work undisturbed.

My father agreed with her. He had a lively sympathy for the predicament of the educated woman who, if she chooses to devote herself to family life instead of a career, "becomes tied to her house, compelled to perform herself a thousand trivial tasks quite unworthy of her ability and training, or, if she does not perform them herself, to ruin her temper by scolding the maids who neglect them."

They did the best they could with the situation in

which they found themselves, but they planned something much better for the future: "good communal housekeeping" and nursery schools run by the state. The "born mothers" could run the nursery schools, and other women could occupy themselves with careers more suited to their characters. It was not clear who was to do what modern feminists call "the shit work," the daily, repetitive labor of cleaning and tidying which takes up so many tedious hours. In those days it was difficult, no matter how much one might theoretically desire it, to imagine a time when the supply of poor and uneducated women available for housework would come to an end.

"The mass of trivial detail" that makes up a housewife's day was not to be inflicted on educated men and women, who were too good for such things, but the care of children was an entirely different matter. It was far too important to be left to inept and ignorant people, no matter how kind, for "there is scarcely a moment passes in a child's life when a mistaken word, gesture or emotion on the part of those in charge of it cannot do untold harm." Warmhearted, uneducated nannies were out of the question; indeed, my mother and father thought that even most parents were not fit to care for their own children without rigorous study of hygiene and child psychology.

My mother recommended most strongly to parents that they educate themselves sufficiently to care for their own children. "Men unhampered by masculine pride and dignity and women without foolish delicacy or feminist bias find all the arduous and trifling activities involved in this task both exciting and delicious. When the child runs in the sunshine or looks up with an intelligent question there stirs in the nature of both parents that bedrock emotion of parental pride—this alert mind—these bright limbs we have made, we ourselves, and shall tend and nurture till we die."

Nevertheless, someone always had charge of us besides our parents, someone supervised bath and bed and morning lessons and nursery meals, and performed many of those arduous and trifling activities that tend to lose their delicious excitement with endless repetition. "Someone" was carefully chosen, young, enlightened and pleasant to have around, but she was not mother or father. They remained free to come and go as they chose, supervising carefully, spending much pleasant time with us, but never absolutely tied down. Either one could go off to America on a lecture tour, leaving us to wait out the desolate weeks of absence in the care of a governess.

That was of course the English upper-class pattern. There was nothing unusual in what they did, except that they saw much more of us than most parents did, and concerned themselves much more deeply with our happiness and welfare. My mother wrote at considerable length about the importance of caring for one's own children; she meant what she said and she acted on her belief, devoting much time to us. Nevertheless, in my memory of those early years she remains little more than one among a number of shadows in the bright light cast by my father.

Once in a while, at Carn Voel, I would wander up to the third floor, where my parents had their bedroom, and sit on the bed watching my mother brush and braid her long brown hair. The sloping attic walls were papered in a black-and-white design like bird footprints, the exposed beams were painted orange, the furniture was white with black and orange trim. A stimulating but rather overwhelming environment, in which she sat before the mirror, looping her lovely hair in braids over her ears, while her silent little daughter watched with fascination. She had brought back from China a folding dressing table of ebony inlaid with mother-of-pearl, with little red-lined drawers for boxes of powder and long strings of amber and ivory beads. It was my special pleasure to investigate all the drawers, then fold down the mirror, close the whole thing for traveling—and open it up again.

A typical little-girl memory, but my only one. Moved by some dim, unconscious resentment of her preoccupation with other things and perhaps by jealousy of her relationship with my father, I armored myself against my mother and tried to forget that I had ever loved her.

My father so dominates my memory that he seems almost the only real live person of my early years. One of the pictures in my album of recollections shows him writing, sitting upright at a small desk, with his back to us, covering page after page with his immaculate handwriting, while we murmured to one another and amused ourselves with reading or drawing or cutting out pictures. Perhaps there were other people in the room as well; I do not remember. My image is of his straight back and the invisible wall of concentration that cut him off from us.

We were not perfectly quiet, of course, and sometimes he would have to admonish us, even suggesting that we would have to leave the room "next time." I do not remember "next time" ever coming, and before too long he would lay down his pen, lean back and say: "There, that's finished. Now you can talk." One morning a week it would be "my Hearst article," and then we were glad, because that didn't take long to write. Week after week for many years he wrote his articles for the Hearst press, along with countless others for all kinds of periodicals, often written in the midst of worry and distraction, though they never showed it. He appeared to be an inexhaustible fountain of wit and wisdom, a tireless purveyor of confident, clear thought.

As children, John and I had a separate life of our own, which came together with that of the adults only at certain times of the day. We had our own room upstairs, a blue-and-white playroom with a view of the sea, where

we did lessons in the mornings, learning from our govern-
esses what are now called "the basic skills" of reading,
writing and numbering, which I learned so young and so
painlessly that I feel I was born knowing them. Looking
back now, recalling our books and toys and pictures, I can
see that our room was most thoughtfully provided with
the things a young child needs to develop hand-eye co-
ordination and elementary concepts of number and size.
We were intellectually privileged children from the very
beginning of our lives.

Apart from lesson time, we spent most of the morning in the garden amusing ourselves. It was a happy place
to play, for the bare, walled field had been transformed by
my mother into a dazzling garden sheltered all round by
a tall hedge of dark green bushes which was her particular
pride. In early days at Carn Voel, when the hedge plants
were still young and tender, they proved irresistible to the
cows in the field outside, who constantly enraged my mother
by munching on her bushes. Once she rushed out in a
fury, waving an umbrella and shouting at the cows in an
attempt to drive them off. Poor little John, who happened
to be in the garden, was terrified and burst into tears.
After much persuasion, and after listening very carefully
and thinking it over for a long time, he finally said:

"Mummy is angry with a cow. John is not a cow."
And he was comforted.

This demonstration of infant reasoning power delighted my father in his philosopher's heart, and he told
the story often—which is how I come to know it, for it
belongs to a time before my memories begin.

John and I spent a lot of time playing ball in the garden, throwing it at the blank end wall of the house and
catching it as it bounced off. The rough surface of the
house sent the ball back at unpredictable angles, making
it hard to catch, but success was worth the effort, as my

father admired such skills. He himself could throw a ball right over the house and he would do it, in the afternoons, for our amusement. Everybody would gather on the lawn to watch, and as soon as the ball was launched into the blue sky John and I would rush round the house to see where it landed and retrieve it. It is not really too difficult to throw a ball over Carn Voel—even I learned to do it when I was older—but if you do not throw hard enough the ball lands on the flat part, where the water tank is, and is lost for good. Remembering how many balls we lost, I begin to think that perhaps my father's skill at throwing was somewhat less than I supposed, though his skill as an entertainer was tremendous.

One of our perennially favorite garden amusements was making "Poison for the Government," a sophisticated variation of the eternal occupation of "messing." My father smoked a pipe; he smoked a pipe for eighty years and was almost never seen without one, except when he was eating or sleeping or shaving. In the pockets of his baggy suit jacket he always had his leather tobacco pouch, a box of matches, a pipe and the little silver instrument for cleaning it, which he called "the three-legged man." It was one of the toys, like his watch, that he used to entertain children.* When he scraped out his pipe, knocked it against the ash tray, filled it with tobacco, tamped it down and lit it with a little wooden match, his clumsy square hands expressed the kindness and gentleness he always showed

---

* His watch was an old gold one on a chain, and he kept it in his vest pocket. For babies, he would hold it by the chain and swing it gently, solemnly intoning "Tick-tock, tick-tock," as their eyes moved to and fro. Older children were shown the face and the winding mechanism, sometimes even the works within the inmost door. Those who were really careful were even allowed to open it themselves, pressing the little levers that made the golden doors spring open. He cherished his watch as he did his Chinese ornaments, respecting their delicate workmanship.

to children. The matchbox also had entertainment value, for he would wedge the pad of his thumb into its opening and then shake his hand so that all the matches rattled. I wanted desperately to be able to do it too, as I always wanted to do whatever he did, but my thumb was too small and its pad too flat, and I always ended up with a box of spilled matches to pick up.

My father had his tobacco sent to him from a shop in London. It came in round tins with a yellow label and it was called Fribourg and Treyer's Golden Mixture. He gave us the empty tins, and we took them outside to make our poison. We put in any kind of garden rubbish we could find: dead leaves, flowers, old grass, twigs, mold, anything that seemed unattractive. Then we went round the back to the water butt, a huge corrugated-iron cylinder of stagnant water, with a tap at the bottom, from which water was drawn for the garden. We added some of this old rain water to our mixture, put on the lid and set it in the sun to ripen. My father suggested, after we had made and labeled a good many tins, that if we called it "Poison for the Government" they would not be likely to drink it. He advised us to call it "Nectar for the Gods," on the ground that this would appeal to their vanity.

Perhaps it seems odd that we amused ourselves with such a gruesome project as planning to kill off the government. Both our parents, however, were born rebels, passionately convinced that everything the government was doing was completely misguided, if not deliberately wicked, and a great deal of their time went to writing and speaking against it, fighting for the rights of the poor, the women, the children and all who had no fighting power of their own. Being progressive parents and anxious to bring up politically intelligent children, they often discussed world affairs with us and told us what they thought. Though we were too young to understand the complexities of the problems, we were certain that the government must be perfectly wrong and should be removed, to make way for intelligent people like our parents, who would run the country properly.

Mornings were for work, afternoons for pleasure, which usually meant going to the beach. "In my memory," my father wrote, "it was always sunny, and always warm after April" in Cornwall. So it was in mine; those early summers present themselves as an endless succession of sunny afternoons spent playing and swimming at the beach while the grownups sat and talked or swam solemnly up and down with their heads stuck out of the water like dignified seals.

There were several possible beaches, each with different advantages. Some had better sand, others better rocks for climbing; some had better streams to dam, others better caves to explore; some were a comparatively short walk from the house, others far enough to require a picnic; some were good at high tide, others at low tide, some were sheltered from the southwest wind, others from the northeast—all factors to be considered and carefully weighed before deciding which beach to go to on a given day.

My favorite beach was Pednevounder, which we called "the Inaccessible" because at first we could find no way down the cliffs to get to it. The Inaccessible was a narrow strip of beach at high tide, with a dark, drippy cave and easy rocks to climb on. At low tide, the unresting Atlantic breakers retreated far out beyond a sandbank and the wide, cool beach ended in a sea pool calm enough for my timorous experiments with swimming. Beyond the beach, rising impregnable out of blue, stood Treen Castle, a tumbled pile of granite, supposed to be the remains of a real castle evilly bewitched. I sat on the sand of the Inaccessible and dreamed of a real Treen Castle in which I was princess and hero, both at the same time. "Inaccessible" to me meant safe, protected from the intruding scorn of older realists. One day I found among its rocks a long, shining sword of silver-painted wood, clear evidence that this beach favored me particularly. I called the sword "Durendal" and played all afternoon at being Roland among the Paladins. I always wanted to go to the Inaccessible, no matter what the tide and weather were doing.

"I do not believe that a sense of justice is innate," my father had written, "but I have been astonished to see how quickly it can be created," provided that it is "real justice" without any "secret bias." He took pains to be fair and to make sure that we were properly aware of his impartiality. When John and I quarreled about which beach to go to, he always settled the argument entirely rationally—but it seemed to me that the rational choice was always in John's favor. Once, finding defeat unbearable, I threw myself down on the hearthrug, howling: "You *always* do what John wants! It's not *fair!*" I knew, even as I screamed, that I was wrong, that he had been fair and my fuss was inexcusable. But what I felt was different: justice always seemed to come out to John's advantage. Gradually I developed a smoldering secret resentment against reason and fairness, and I came to feel that life itself was unfair, favoring John at my expense.

"If you are fonder of some of the children than of others, you must be on your guard to prevent your affections from having any influence on your distribution of pleasures," my father warned, and he was careful to heed his own warning. But that did not prevent me from suspecting that a preference existed. John was two years older than I, articulate, charming, an incessant talker and the center of everyone's attention. I worshipped him from the beginning and took it for granted that he was in every way my superior and would be better liked by family and friends. Most of the time I was quite willing to keep my mouth shut and take second place; indeed, I found a certain safety in my position in the shadows.

"What are you thinking, Kate?" people would ask, seeing a faraway look in my eyes.

"Oh, nothing"—a hasty cover-up for the shapeless ignorance of my thoughts, not to be compared with the intellectual brilliance of John's or my parents'.

Under my surface humility, however, ran a strong undercurrent of arrogant resentment, which only rarely burst out into the sort of open scene my father deplored. Usually it contented itself with undermining John's position by demonstrating my superior virtue, wherever this could be done without open competition. When he was overexcited, I was stolid; when he showed fear, I became intrepid; if he grew muddled about anything, I struggled to master it perfectly while modestly almost concealing my knowledge. I waged a cruel campaign against John, imagining him invulnerable in his superior strength. When I became aware that I could harm him, I tried to stop, but the unpleasant habit of secret competition had by then gained a hold upon me, and I have never been able to shake it off completely. Poor John, trapped between his parents' high expectations and his sister's bitter rivalry, must have felt unable to please anyone and quite alone in a difficult world.

None of this was apparent on those long sunny Cornish afternoons, during which John and I lived the immediate life of children, responding to cues of weather and environment and people without any awareness that life could be otherwise. We rejoiced in the physical pleasures of summer: hot sand and cold water, the everlasting battle of ocean against granite, the golden light and long shadows of late afternoon, the satisfaction of good food and long sleep. We enjoyed every benefit our parents had hoped to provide, and for us the Cornish idyll was real, though imperfect.

When time was short or the weather uncertain, we would walk to Porthcurno beach, the closest, which lay a mile down the valley from our house, beyond the village of Porthcurno, to which Carn Voel belonged. The road went down past the post office, the shop and the dark garage, then on past a row of fine bay-windowed houses set in neat gardens behind neat hedges and well-painted gates, an incongruous sight in that rural setting. These villas had been built by the Cable Company to house its officials, who worked in a big building humming with machinery farther down the road. Porthcurno, the English end of the transatlantic cable, had once been a busy place, and it remained the shadow of a company village. Carn Voel itself was the work of the company, a boardinghouse built as compensation for the widow of an employee lost at sea off a Cable Company ship. The inhabitants of the villas in the valley carried their own way of life with them like a protective covering: tennis courts, lawns, neat gravel drives, tea in the garden and all the rest of it. The kind of life made familiar in countless English detective stories.

Though they lived year round in Porthcurno, the Cable Company people never belonged there any more than we did; they were English foreigners, not true Cornishmen. We came to know some of the local people as tradesmen or as servants, and a few became lifelong friends of my mother's. Especially Matt and Daisy, who worked for us in the garden and in the house. They were small and brown and beautiful, and Matt, with his dark curly hair and merry eyes, was my first, most secret love. He did our gardening and pumped our water, and he was the local postman, riding about on his bike in uniform, with a heavy leather satchel over his shoulder. Once, comfortably settled in the pub, Matt refused to heed the call of duty and to set out upon his rounds.

"Matt, you have to go," they said.

"I'm not going," he said.

"But it's your duty!"

"I don't care."

"You owe it to the GPO" (the General Post Office).

"I'm not going."

"It's your duty to your king and country."

"I don't care for the GPO, nor me king and country neither," said Matt—a statement that endeared him to my parents but almost cost him his post-office job.

With such local people we had friendly, though restricted, relations. With the local respectable gentry we had nothing to do at all. Our ties to Cornwall were with the place, not the people, and the lively visitors who swarmed about Carn Voel were all imported. Not that my mother and father ever did anything deliberately to antagonize their respectable neighbors. Though publicly fearless in the face of bigotry, privately they liked a quiet life, and though they taught us children to despise conventional opinions, they also taught us never to flaunt our contempt in the faces of those who held them. It would have been rude and inconsiderate; furthermore, it might have involved us in painful conflict, and they hoped to spare us that. Because they could afford to live an isolated, independent life and, later, to create their own school, it was possible for them to realize this hope; John and I were well protected from the oppression of respectability, while its upholders were spared the distress of perceiving our uncouthness.

I'm not sure whether, in the long run, this was a good thing. I grew up with an exaggerated awe of respectable people, which made it difficult for me to fit into the everyday world. I felt that everything I said and did naturally would shock people and that I had better, for my own protection, attempt to conform to my parents' stereotype of conventional wisdom. Like the cat who walked by himself, I prized my independence and my freedom to walk in the wet wild woods alone; but also, like the cat, I coveted the warm security of ordinary life, for which a considerable sacrifice of eccentricity seemed necessary. Walking past the villas of Porthcurno as a child, odd in my boy's clothes, free to say and to do so many things forbidden to the young of those houses, I felt that their disapproval might shoot out in a hot blast and shrivel me on sight. It always seemed wisest to creep by unnoticed. Of course I needn't have been so cowardly, but, like my father, I have always preferred to avoid conflict and embarrassment on a personal level. And our comfortable isolation was very pleasant while it lasted; John and I were never torn by the conflicting demands of home and society, as my children have been in attempting the impossible task of pleasing friends and school and parents all at the same time.

At the bottom of Porthcurno valley, the road goes off up the hill to St. Levan, while a footpath leads on through the tangled undergrowth to the beach. The path ends in sand and rock and coarse sea grass, and tangles of rusty barbed wire strung across the beach in the First World War, in case the Germans should try to land and attack the cable station.

We left our shoes in the grass at the top of the beach, then jumped, ran, rolled, tumbled or walked sedately down a steep sand slope to the beach proper. That slope was the first trial on the long way home, steep and slippery and hard for tired children to climb: one step forward and two steps back, it seemed to me. My father called this place "the Gobi Desert," and he would tell us about the great Gobi Desert in China as we climbed, making it a little easier, but not much.

Once down on the beach, we stood and discussed the serious matter of where to settle. It was important to find a place in the sun and out of the wind. While the tall cliffs on either side of the beach afforded good protection from the wind, they also cut off the sun, and the shady side of the beach grew chilly in the afternoon. There was the tide to consider too: if it was going out, we settled as close to the water as the sand was dry; if it was coming in, we settled well back from the water, so as not to risk losing our equipment to an unexpectedly big wave. Cornish waves come sailing in from across the wide Atlantic; far out to sea, they are as sleek as a porpoise's back, but when they come to land they gather themselves up like tigers and leap upon the beach with a roar, sweeping round in a fan of sandy foam and scooping treasures back with them into deep water. We got a wicked pleasure from seeing inexperienced beachgoers scrambling to gather up their stuff in the face of the oncoming tide.

So did my children, a generation later. I remember a man in suit and shoes, smoking a pipe, in the middle of the beach and watching the waves. Up came an extra-large one and soaked him to the knees. "That was a dirty one!" he exclaimed; with commendable dignity. My children were enchanted by his misfortune and his poise, and the exclamation passed into our family folklore.

After long discussion, we would choose a place in the sun, not too far from the water, with some flat rocks to put things on, then peel off our clothes and head for the water, John and I at breakneck speed, the grownups walking, as they always do. I never could understand why they sat and talked so much at the beach, when there were so many other wonderful things to do. Was it possible that they didn't want to dig holes and build castles, to climb up the rocks and jump into soft sand or cold water? Secretly I rather despised their inertia.

My father swam up and down the beach breast stroke, with his red face and white hair sticking up out of the water. Then he would turn on his back and make a won-

derful fountain for us by kicking with his legs. My mother,
who was more daring, dived off an old diving board someone had fastened to a high rock at one side of the beach,
and she swam much farther out.

My father taught us to swim, and to be wisely cautious without being timid. Cornish beaches can be very
dangerous if you don't know them: the water is usually
rough (and very cold), the sand may shelve steeply, there
is a wicked undertow and often the currents can quickly
carry you beyond reach of help. There were of course no
lifeguards, so we were responsible for our own safety. He
taught us to stay close to shore, to pay attention to the
tide, to be aware of currents, to float in on top of a wave
instead of struggling with the undertow beneath. He was a
good teacher; we learned to respect the water without
timidity and we never got into serious difficulty.

When we had had enough of the water, we went
climbing on the rocks. There were granite cliffs and boulders
and caves to explore at every beach, and John became a
bold and skillful climber. I usually went only far enough
to find a warm and secret ledge where I could sit and
dream, though sometimes I climbed like John, going up
and up for the excitement of it, hoping to be able to reach
the grass at the top of the cliff. A foolish ambition, because beyond the grass were heather and gorse and other
prickly things quite hard to negotiate without shoes and
clothes. Once, on such an expedition, I arrived on a sloping rock slippery with gravel and there I stuck, afraid to
move. I yelled for my father, who came up and told me
where to put my feet and calmly helped me down. He
didn't usually climb on rocks himself, unless it was necessary to get down to a beach, and I thought that was just
part of his grownupness. Not until I was grown myself did
I discover that he feared heights, which made him dizzy.
When I then remembered how calmly he let us climb

where we could, how coolly he helped me out of my predicament, I belatedly admired his courage and his self-
control. Of course we might have fallen and been seriously
hurt; we might have gone off somewhere and been caught
by the tide while they sat and talked. But we didn't. We
were allowed to do what we were able to do and not be
afraid.

Once when we were visiting my father in Wales I
took my children to visit Harlech Castle, a medieval for-
tress on a rock above a wide estuary. We went up and up
the spiral staircase, anticipating the view from the battlements over fields and villages to the distant mountains of
Snowdonia—but when we came out on top we found there
was no wall; we could look straight over the edge to the
courtyard far below! I had never been afraid of heights
before, but up there with my children, picturing one of
them stumbling over the edge, I panicked and grew dizzy
and hurried them quickly down again. Then I understood
how my father, a daring mountaineer in his youth, came
to suffer from vertigo and to stay away from heights. But
he concealed it better than I, letting his children take
chances and learn things despite his own fear.

Every beach had a cave, a cold, dark crack leading back
into the cliff, with water dripping from above and slimy,
seaweed-covered boulders on the floor. My father once
said that if you went far enough into a cave you might
come to a vacuum, which John took to be some kind of
monster, like a dragon. This funny idea of John's was
spoken of with such amusement that I never liked to admit
that I didn't exactly know what a vacuum was myself.

It was rather awful being the youngest in my father's
household, never quite sure if things were fact or fiction
and always afraid to ask. When I was very young, my father told me that Hungary used to be called "Yumyum"
but that they changed it to Hungary because they thought

it was more dignified. He told us both, when we slurped our soup, that King Ludwig of Bavaria used to do that and his courtiers had him locked up as insane. Was it true? There was a mad King Ludwig of Bavaria, of course, but did he bubble in his soup? Had my father made it all up or had he read it somewhere in some out-of-the-way book, of the sort he so often discovered? I never asked him, and now I shall never know.

The worst story, though, was about the Duke of Wellington's tail. My father told us one day that the Duke of Wellington had had a very small tail, which did not usually show under his coat, though he had to have a special hole made in his saddle in order to be comfortable on a horse. This sounded quite plausible to me, so I filed it away among the many facts of history I gleaned from my father's conversation. Some years later, after I had gone away to boarding school, I studied the period of the Napoleonic Wars in history. Anxious to share my special knowledge, I assured the teacher that the Iron Duke had had a tail: my father had told me so, and his grandparents had known the Duke. The teacher remained skeptical, so I applied to my father for confirmation. First he smiled, then he laughed, then he said "Well . . . ," and I lost a beautiful illusion, along with a fragment of my faith in my father.

His grandmother had indeed known the Duke of Wellington, and disapproved of him too, and I think she must have been the source of the many malicious stories my father used to tell about him.

My father used to say that, in his grandmother's view, everything that had happened before the Napoleonic Wars was history, whereas everything since was gossip. These stories, samples of the gossip, were invaluable in making history come alive for us, even when they were not true.

Every year on April Fool's Day my father used to look

out of the window and exclaim: "Goodness gracious, there's an elephant coming up the garden path!" And year after year he managed to convince me, even though I knew I had been fooled the year before, even though I knew it was impossible. He was always so utterly plausible. Perhaps, after all, it is not surprising that my confidence in my own grasp on reality was rather small.

When I was very young, he used to pretend sometimes that I was "Miss Wogglywoo" and not Kate at all.

"No, I'm not Miss Wogglywoo," I would reply. "I'm Kate."

"Oh, you must be mistaken. You don't look a bit like Kate."

"I *am* Kate. I'm *not* Miss Wogglywoo!"

"Dear me, you don't say so! No, no, you can't be Kate. You're Miss Wogglywoo."

"No, I'm *not!* I'm Kate! Can't you see?"

"Well, let me have a good look at you. No, Kate doesn't have eyes like that. That's not Kate's hair. You must be Miss Wogglywoo."

"No, no! I'm *not* Miss Wogglywoo! I'm KATE!" And I would burst into tears, desperately afraid it might be true, terrifyingly uncertain of my own identity.

But almost all his teases were perfectly good-natured, though often confusing. I can remember only one other that upset me, and I doubt if he ever realized it. When I did anything tiresome he would quote from James Stephens's *Crock of Gold*: " 'Daughters,' said the philosopher, 'have been a trouble to their parents since the world began.' " The quotation really hurt. I wanted never ever to be a trouble to him and I hated that pronouncement, which made it seem so inevitable that I would be.

Almost every beach had a stream as well as a cave, a stream that ran peat brown from the bogs on the high ground and lost itself in the sand before it reached the sea. When the tide was very high and the weather had been very wet, sometimes stream and sea would meet, but not often. We spent hours building dams for the streams with stones and sand, trying to see how long we could hold back the water and how big we could make the pool behind the dam. My father, an expert dam adviser, stood there with his pipe, pointing out weak spots, which John and I would rush to reinforce with frantic scoops of sand. Finally the dam would break, beginning with a tiny trickle over the top, which spread into a stream as the dam cracked under it, till at last a brown torrent rushed to the sea, cutting new sand cliffs and eroding old ones as it ran. Playing with dams was fun. It also taught us a good deal of geology in a practical sort of way. My father was such a learned man in so many fields and so interested in everything that he couldn't help teaching us something in almost everything we did, from how to choose a safe branch when climbing a tree to the origins of Indo-European. Often enough I understood half or less of what he said, but as I went on in school I found that almost everything was an old friend that at last I understood, rather than a stranger whose measure had to be taken. There was, for instance, the matter of the shadows cast by the lamps we used at Carn Voel. There was no electricity in the house then, so in the downstairs rooms we used oil lamps with white globes and silk shades, which gave a lovely light. My father pointed out to us that the lamp and its shade described a parabola or a hyperbola on the wall. Having no idea what these were, I supposed they were simply the names for the shapes of light and shade that a lamp makes on a wall. I was quite surprised when I met them again in mathematics.

One of the beaches we liked to go to was St. Levan, in the next valley to Porthcurno. To get there, we walked along a footpath through the fields from our house to St.

Levan church, then across the road and down another path
to the beach. There were so many footpaths and lanes
around the house that we rarely had to walk along the
roads.

The path beyond St. Levan church led only to the
beach and the cliffs 'above it. On its way down the valley
this path passed St. Levan rectory, a fine house, in a me-
ticulous garden, with wide sparkling windows looking out
to the sea. I peeped through the hedge as we walked by
below the garden, half-hoping to see its splendid inhabitants strolling on the lawn before going in to elegant
afternoon tea in spacious rooms filled with heavy furniture
and muffled by thick carpets and heavy curtains. Had there
ever been anyone on the lawn to return my furtive stare,
I should have longed for the cloak of darkness to hide my
oddity from their contempt. '

My parents regarded the Church of England as a
monster of power and wealth lying sluggishly across the
path of progress and callously destroying the happiness of
all who could not or would not live by its doctrines. Christianity meant to them a life-denying puritan faith, which
would sacrifice all present happiness to the hope of celes-
tial reward—and would impose a similar style of life even
on those who did not share its beliefs. The Church of
England was obviously, in their eyes, corrupted by wealth
and power and slothfulness, and yet it continued hypocrit-
ically to enforce standards of public behavior that even its
own members found hard to maintain. Their bitterness
against church influence in education and morals was intense, the more so because they were convinced of its ability to preserve the unpleasant *status quo* into the forsee-
able future.

All this reactionary power and smug cruelty were rep-
resented by St. Levan rectory, sunning itself so comfortably
among its lovely flowers. No wonder that I regarded it with

fear! Yet at the same time it had an awful fascination,
looking so comfortable, so safe, so well tended; it was the
visible expression of the power structure, to use a modern
phrase, and I felt vaguely that if I could get inside there
and *belong* I might cease to be afraid. Within the house
lived possessors of a magic powerful against the wild
chances of life, and those they welcomed into the charmed
circle might share their protection. But I could not be one
of them, for I was a part of the enemy, exposed not only
to the normal risks of living but also to their powerful disapproval, and could not wish it otherwise, knowing they
were both wicked and foolish.

Many years later, in an entirely different life, my husband and I went with our children as missionaries to
Uganda. On our way back to America, we stopped to visit
my mother in Cornwall and went on Sunday to the local
parish church, as proper Christians should. After the service
we spoke to the rector, who was impressed by our missionary service and invited us to tea. So at last I came to
see the inside of that formidable and seductive house. It
was small when you got inside, awkwardly planned and
sadly dilapidated. The lovely garden had all run wild.
Clearly the rectory family had a hard time making ends
meet and maintaining in proper style the house they lived
in. Where was the comfortable security I had so envied?
Had it always been an illusion or had the balance of power
shifted in the years I had been away? I felt I had chosen
the wrong side again and was still, as always, a loser.

My parents had grown up inside the system. They had
had stability and permanence, far more of it than they
wanted. Stable institutions and permanent rules thwarted
them in every direction, and they longed for change. Their
feet were firm on the ground of the accepted truth with
which they had been brought up, even when they rejected
it, and this gave them strength. We, on the other hand,

were raised in opposition. We never belonged to a stable society or made our own escape at our own time, on our own terms. I have not enjoyed this isolation and I have spent my life searching for a place to belong, but without success. For me, there is no permanence in the world outside of Cornwall, except in the knowledge that the whole shifting, turning universe rests in the hands of a God more durable than the granite cliffs of Land's End.

The stream that ran down St. Levan beach passed by the rectory garden, and the path went across it on a stone-slab bridge. In the clear brown water under the bridge we could see the rectory potato peelings, cast there for some reason of laziness or convenience, and they would prompt my father to deliver himself of a sermon, the only occasion on which I have heard him preach. The sermon went like this:

> *Dearly beloved brethren, is it not a sin,*
> *When we peel potatoes, to throw away the skin?*
> *For the skin feeds the pigs and the pigs feed you.*
> *Dearly beloved brethren, is this not true?*

It seems to me that only a God with a sense of humor could have brought together my father and the sermon and the clerical potato peelings at the same point in time and space.

Cornwall is warmer than many parts of England, but it can hardly be considered hot; if the temperature ever reached ninety, people would surely be prostrated by the heat. Yet John and I, as children, spent whole afternoons with nothing on, constantly in and out of the water, and I do not remember being cold. My mother believed that people should be tough and uncomplaining, so that they could get on with the business of enjoying life in all kinds of circumstances. "The person of steadiest judgment about his own needs and the needs of others," she said, "will be the child who has been brought up hard, but without want." She did her best to make sure that we acquired steady judgment in this way. The only real discomfort I remember from the summertime was sunburn, for me an annual misery. We wore hats for fear of sunstroke and shoes for fear of tetanus, but sunburn was not considered serious enough to be worth preventing. I used to reflect gloomily, as my mother rubbed my sore back and arms with olive oil, that John's comfortable dark skin was just another proof of his natural superiority and life's favoritism.

Being tough and uncomplaining included taking a good deal of responsibility for ourselves. We carried our own stuff to the beach and back, and any treasures we found there we had to get home for ourselves if we wanted them. Once, at Nanjizal, a beach so far from home that it took all our strength to get there and back, John found a beautiful stone, which he very much wanted to keep. Nanjizal had unusually lovely stones, a profusion of rounded boulders of many colors, which it seemed a pity to leave there unadmired. But they were far too heavy to carry. Though John's was comparatively small, it was clearly beyond his strength.

"You'll have to carry it yourself, John," they said.

"Won't you help me?" John said. "It's such an extra-beautiful stone."

"No," they said. "If you want it, John, you must carry it."

So we set out up the steep hill that began the way home, John huffing and struggling under his ever heavier load. At last he could manage it no longer and had to give up, unable to persuade anyone to help him with it. I felt terribly sorry for him, understanding perfectly the wound to his pride, as well as his grief over losing the stone. I think I would have carried it for him if I could; though at the same time I felt he had been foolish to try. He should have realized that the grownups always knew best.

Were they wise or cruel or both? Memory says they

were cruel: the challenge was too great, and John learned humiliation and despair, not self-reliance and resourcefulness. But memory does not tell me how they felt, how they suffered with John, how gladly they would have helped him if they had not thought it important not to. When no principle was involved, my father was eager to help us in difficulties, to make our lives as pleasant as possible—coming home from Porthcurno beach, for example. Going to the beach, John and I would run ahead and back like a pair of dogs, picking flowers, watching cows and horses, scrambling up the steep banks beside the road to walk along the top of them, high above the earth-bound adults. Coming home was not so easy. First the scramble up the Gobi Desert, then the long uphill walk along the hot tarred road when we were tired and hungry. To help us along, my father invented wonderful stories, which he told as we walked. My favorite was an endless serial about the flying post office of Pinky Ponk Tong, which looked just like Porthcurno post office, square and solid and rooted to the ground; but with wings made of postage stamps that carried it off to such fabulous places as Semipalatinsk, where it had remarkable adventures. Besides its amazing ability to fly all over the world, that post office had a very real magic power: it could shrink a long, hot, uphill mile to almost nothing.

Looking back on the sunny Cornish summers of my childhood is like looking through the wrong end of a telescope. Far away and very small, a family sits on a beach in the sunshine against a background of sparkling blue-green sea. As I try to describe what I see, clouds keep passing over the sun, darkening the picture with fleeting shadows. In my memory, as in my father's, there is only sunshine, until I start recalling details. Of course there were griefs and tensions and problems; they are as natural to living as shadows are to sunlight. But they were small then, or we thought they were—only little chilly pauses in the summer's warmth. Most days were truly warm and happy, even when the wind blew and the rain fell and beaches were out of the question.

"The beauty of the Cornish coast is inextricably mixed in my memories with the ecstasy of watching two healthy happy children learning the joys of sea and rocks and sun and storm," wrote my father in his *Autobiography*. For me, its beauty will always be mixed inextricably with the happiness of his love. In every month of every summer, on every beach of my childhood, he stands in the center of the picture in the sunshine, the very image of love. He stands on the sand with his feet turned out like a dancing master, wearing a long white shirt, whose tails reach almost to his knees, and a Panama hat. He looks a little like a cockatoo, with his great red nose, always peeling in summer, his white hair and his sharply twinkling eyes. He is holding a pipe in his hand and telling a witty story, which he finishes with a deafening burst of hearty laughter, looking quizzically at his listeners to see if they share his amusement. I sit on the sand, quietly making designs with my hand or arranging shells, and I watch him with absorbing love as he entertains his adult audience. He looks to me like a sort of summer Santa Claus, the red-faced, cheerful embodiment of kindness and generosity. Incoherently, I feel what a privilege it is to have this great man for a father, and I promise myself never, ever, to do anything to distress him.

Ancient History

Life began well for my father: he was born to prosperous
and remarkably enlightened parents, who loved each other
and their children very much. His father had the old Russell
sense of obligation to England, remarkably high principles
and some very radical ideas. His mother, a Stanley, shared
her family's immense vitality and her husband's advanced
ideas. They had money enough and could therefore devote
themselves to the nurture of their children and the promo-
tion of the causes dear to their hearts, such as the emancipation of women. Kate Stanley seems to have been a sensible and affectionate woman, unsentimentally devoted to
her husband and three children. Unluckily, when my father
was only two she died of diphtheria, caught while nursing
his older brother and sister. His sister, Rachel, died too,
while his desolate father survived for little more than a
year. Nothing remained of the child's first happiness except
remote, half-conscious recollections of love and a lifelong
yearning for its recovery.

After his father's death, my father went to live with
his grandmother Russell at Pembroke Lodge, a house of
shadows and hushed voices, of age and anxiety and invalid-

ism. He was "rescued" to this environment by legal action, for his freethinking parents had left their children to the care of freethinking guardians, to whom the grandparents felt they could not possibly entrust those innocent boys. Frank, who was seven years older, rebelled bitterly and was sent away to school; but dear little Bertie was gathered into the sentimental austerity of his grandmother's house and showered with her destructive love. She believed that plain food, uncomfortable living and unceasing moral exhortation mixed with reproach were good for boys. She had brought up her own children that way and felt that their upright moral character demonstrated the rightness of her methods. My grandfather Amberley was a neurotic prig and something of a nervous invalid all his short life. His brother Willy went mad and spent most of his long life in an asylum. Aunt Agatha had to break off her engagement because of insane delusions, and she remained at home as her mother's devoted shadow. Uncle Rollo was so shy he hardly dared to speak to anyone but children. But these, in Grandmother Russell's eyes, were all misfortunes of heredity; she had no idea that her heavy emphasis on guilt, duty and gratitude might be a contributing cause. Rather, she supposed she was doing what she could to counteract the effects of "bad blood." Grandmother Russell died many, many years before I was born, yet I have always felt a particular and personal dislike for her, because of the misery she caused my father.

All through his childhood, my father submitted humbly and gratefully to her reproofs and admonitions, and regretted sadly his inability to live up to her high expectations. From the age of four until he was almost ready for the university, he lived as the only child in that house of melancholy adults, in a solitude broken only by occasional visits and trips away from home. At first the kindliness of his grandfather comforted him, but Lord John Russell was old by then, at the end of his life, sitting in a Bath chair in the sunshine and looking backward into the past; within two years he was dead. Though his childhood was probably not quite as awful as his memory painted it, nevertheless it was bad enough to burden my father with a lifelong sense of sin and a sad feeling of isolation. In adolescence, his loneliness became so frantic that he thought he must be going mad, and it was not until he went to Cambridge that he met like-minded people and realized he was not a freak.

The years at Cambridge liberated my father. He met "all the best minds" of his day, engaged in long arguments and even longer walks, and made many devoted lifelong friends. This caused his grandmother no concern. She had little interest in things of the mind and did not feel herself in competition with intellectual young men. When he decided to get married, however, that was an entirely different matter.

Grandmother Russell was always upset by marriages in the family. When my grandfather Amberley wanted to marry Kate Stanley, she raised as many objections as she possibly could, sensing, quite rightly, that Kate would not be a suitably submissive daughter-in-law. Thirty years later, she met the same challenge all over again with her grandson, and in a far worse form. Dear Bertie was barely twenty-one, a mere child, totally innocent of the world, and he wanted to marry Alys Pearsall-Smith, an American five years older than himself.

She sighed over him and reproached him; she suggested that Alys was a fortune hunter, a baby snatcher, was not a lady. Aunt Agatha begged him to consider his grandmother's health and not to bring down her grey hairs with sorrow to the grave.

Then Grandmother Russell played her trump card: she got the family doctor to tell him all about Aunt Agatha and Uncle Willy, to reveal to him that his own father had had epilepsy (probably this was a mistake), to remind him that Alys had a quite peculiar uncle; with such a heritage on both sides, he must expect his children to be doomed, should he be so foolhardy as to go ahead with the marriage. This was a heavy blow. He deeply desired children, and at the same time he passionately loved Alys. They decided to marry, but to practice birth control, a scandalous procedure his grandmother had not even contemplated. It was not much of a sacrifice for Alys, but for my father it was a terrible choice. Fear of madness hung over Pembroke Lodge like a family curse; an inherited evil that might appear without warning, even after years of apparent sanity. In his anguished conflict, my father suffered from appalling nightmares, which caused him to fear for his own sanity and left him with a horror of madness that later made it extremely difficult for him to deal competently with the breakdown of his eldest son.

When my father came of age, he came into money of his own; he was free to marry at last and would yield neither to threats nor to tears. So Grandmother Russell and Aunt Agatha put the best face on it they could and treated Alys with acid sweetness, never missing an opportunity to make her uncomfortable in their own gentle, backhanded way. And my father married, at the age of twenty-one, a beautiful woman whom he had loved devotedly since his first sight of her, when he was only seventeen and almost too shy to speak.

In the first volume of my father's *Autobiography* there is a picture of him taken in 1893, the year he married Alys. What an innocent youth! Butter wouldn't melt in his mouth. His eyes look out calmly beneath a smooth and noble forehead. There is no discord in this face, no hint of doubt or uncertainty; the face of one who knows the highest ideals and follows them without question. The name of

Galahad, which Grandmother Russell had wished to inflict on the poor baby, would be quite appropriate to this young man. Looking at the picture and reading his early letters, I am reminded of Walter Pater's phrase "to burn always with this hard, gemlike flame." I do not recognize my father in the letters or in the picture.

At the outset of his marriage, my father had no financial worries, interesting work to do, plenty of congenial friends and a much-loved wife. He also had a conviction that he had a contribution to make to philosophy important enough to justify several years of "selfish," single-minded devotion to his own work. This is the happy point at which novels end but marriages begin. As the first romance faded, however, it was not replaced by a steady affection, nor by the common interest that children might have provided.* I wonder sometimes how powerful his longing for children was in diminishing his love for Alys. Though they appeared to share a congenial common life, he was so absorbed in his arduous philosophical labors that he did not notice how that life had changed until, as he wrote, "I went out bicycling one afternoon, and suddenly, as I was riding along a country road, I realized that I no longer loved Alys. I had had no idea until this moment that my love for her was even lessening."

I have never really been able to believe this story. It hardly seems possible for anyone to be so totally unaware of his feelings toward someone with whom he shares an intimate daily life. Yet he was plainly unaware of being aware of them. Change seemed to grow inside him slowly, gathering force until it burst forth like. a volcano, obliterating all that had gone before. When he ceased to love a woman, he ceased to love her totally, and usually he wanted no more to do with her. He could be a devoted,

---

* After a year or two away from the lugubrious atmosphere of Pembroke Lodge, they had decided that it would be quite safe to have children after all, only to discover that Alys was barren.

lifelong, generous friend to men, but his relations with women were always more complex and less satisfactory. His friendships were like warm and steady fires, and they gave great pleasure; his loves were as spectacular as fireworks and often as brief, and their souvenir was a burnt black shell. Unfortunately, this burnt shell was sometimes a woman who could not stop loving him just because he had ceased to find his ideal in her.

Having concluded that he no longer loved Alys, he did not know what to do next. Honesty compelled him to tell her how he felt, while kindness forbade him to leave her without more cause. So they continued together for nine years, sharing a house and a misery but nothing more. Had he not fallen in love with Ottoline Morrell, it's possible they might have stayed together many further years.

But he did fall in love with Ottoline. She was glamorous, exotic, aristocratic, artistic, everything that Quaker Alys was not, and he had known her slightly, disapprovingly, for many years. In the course of working for her husband's re-election to Parliament, he came to know her better and to respect her character. During an accidental evening tête-à-tête in London, he came to know her even better; as the evening progressed, they gradually overcame their shyness and "I found to my amazement that I loved her deeply, and that she returned my feeling."

Full of the joy of his grand new passion, he demanded his freedom from Alys, who suddenly grew angry, after her years of patient endurance, and refused to let him go. "After she had stormed for some hours," he wrote, "I gave a lesson in Locke's philosophy to her niece . . . who was about to take her Tripos. I then rode away on my bicycle, and with that my first marriage came to an end. I did not see Alys again till 1950."

I remember my stepmother, many, many years later, referring to his bicycle departure with a mixture of joking and apprehension. If he had still had a bicycle, she would have been frantic with worry! She was always anxious when he went off by himself, lest he should return to announce a total change of heart—or, worse still, decide not to return at all. Sometimes it was rather absurd. He spent much of his time sitting in an armchair reading, spectacles on his nose and pipe in his hand. Then, in the course of nature, he would get up to go to the bathroom. He always jumped up suddenly, without a word, and hurried out of the room. She would look up in alarm and ask: "Where are you going?"

"To the bathroom."

"Oh, all right . . ."

He could not be tied down, but he was not ruthless either. The coldly correct unkindness with which he treated Alys after he ceased to love her was in no way deliberate. His self-control was of such heroic proportions that, having decided on the right behavior for a situation, he was usually able to act on his decision, or at least to appear to do so.

According to my father, Ottoline began his transformation into the man I remember. He came to her puritanical, priggish, self-righteous, convinced that only his iron self-discipline kept his natural wickedness under control. She laughed at him. She surrounded herself with beautiful objects and delicious perfumes, which worked strongly on his senses once he had got over his disapproval of them. He began to believe that life contains other pleasures besides the rewards of virtue. But there were appalling complications. Alys and her brother continued to rage, while Ottoline would not leave her husband and child, so there was rarely a chance for the lovers to enjoy their affection in peace. And the affection itself was not exactly restful. "In your presence I am always paralyzed with terror, stiff and awkward from the sense of your criticism. I know that some things I do or don't do annoy you, for reasons I don't understand, and it makes it impossible for me to be natural before you, though sometimes it makes me exaggerate the things you hate."

Ottoline was different from his other loves, because he was in awe of her. Perhaps she was the last woman he looked up to, as the child had looked up to his grandmother. Unusually for him, he maintained a steady affection for Ottoline for many years after they ceased to be lovers, and this may have been because she was never wholeheartedly his; she had her own life, one he could not destroy.

The happiness my father had learned from Ottoline was soon darkened and almost destroyed by the coming of the First World War. He had grown up with an optimistic Victorian belief in automatic progress, with confidence that the whole world would, in its own good time, follow the wise course of the English from ancient brutality to civilized self-government. Then, suddenly, he found his own beloved compatriots dancing in the streets at the prospect of slaughtering great numbers of fellow human beings who happened to speak German.

He fought the folly and the cruelty all through the war, determined that kindliness and reason should not be totally eclipsed. He cherished and fought for the young conscientious objectors as though they had been his own sons—as indeed they might have been had his first marriage proved fruitful—and he grieved over the wholesale slaughter of the young men who felt it their duty to fight. His frantic grief over the sufferings of war induced in him a contempt for its supporters every bit as strong as theirs for him. In the First World War, as again in Vietnam, his skeptical intelligence gave way before his passionate identification with the agony of mankind.

The grief my father endured in the face of the lunatic sufferings of the First War was to some extent relieved by his love for Colette O'Niel, whom he met through his work for the conscientious objectors. I can remember Colette from occasional visits she made to us during the years at Beacon Hill School. She wore glamorous trailing clothes, strings and strings of long beads and quantities of perfume, and she always brought exotic gifts. When she and my father first met, she was a young and beautiful actress, passionately against the war. They clung to one another in desperation, feeling themselves an island of love in a sea of hate, and gradually he transferred to Colette the wholehearted devotion Ottoline had been unwilling to reciprocate. It was a bittersweet love affair: private ecstasy mixed with public anguish, heights of confident joy alternating with depths of utter hopelessness, and all wrought up to the highest intensity by the background agony of the war.

Though Colette and Ottoline were two of the great loves of my father's life, they were by no means the only ones. Having given up strict monogamy with the end of his first marriage, he no longer felt any need to restrict his affections, which he distributed most liberally throughout the rest of his life.

When I studied Goethe, in college, the professor taught us to connect each creative burst with a new love affair: Goethe drew the life of his poetry from his loves, then moved on and left them. Sometimes I think my father was like that. Perhaps it is a characteristic of great men, who must follow their gift regardless of consequences. And he says himself: "I have known no woman to whom the claims of intellect were as absolute as they are to me, and wherever intellect intervened, I have found that the sympathy I sought in love was apt to fail."

He never gave his whole heart to anyone, though he tried. "My most profound feelings have remained always solitary and have found in human things no companionship," he wrote. "The sea, the stars, the night wind in waste places, mean more to me than even the human beings I love best, and I am conscious that human affection is to me at bottom an attempt to escape from the vain search for God."

We who loved him were secondary to the sea and stars and the absent God; we were not loved for ourselves, but as bridges out of loneliness. We were part of a charade of togetherness acted by a fundamentally solitary person. He played at being a father in the same way, and he acted the part to perfection, but his heart was elsewhere and his combination of inner detachment and outer affection caused me much muddled suffering.

"The War of 1914–1918 changed everything for me," wrote my father. "I ceased to be academic and took to writing a new kind of books. I changed my whole conception of human nature. I became for the first time deeply convinced that Puritanism does not make for human happiness. Through the spectacle of death I acquired a new love for what is living. I became convinced that most human beings are possessed by a profound unhappiness venting itself in destructive rages, and that only through the diffusion of instinctive joy can a good world be brought into being." By the end of the war he "had got rid of the don and the Puritan" and had become the man most of us remember: a combination of jolly entertainer and tireless crusader for constructive social reforms, as well as a brilliant and famous philosopher.

In 1915 my father composed a course of lectures later published as *Principles of Social Reconstruction*. A book unlike any that had gone before, but very much like a great deal that he wrote subsequently. One can almost read it as a program for his postwar life and writings. He writes of the state, of war and education, marriage and religion, in just the way I so often heard him speak at home. These are the ideas I grew up with.

Especially interesting to me is his chapter on education, written before he had any hope of children of his own or any personal reason to concern himself with the subject. A large part of his educational theory was set out here, a good six years before he had a child to try it on; an intellectual ideal of how one ought to treat children in order to have them turn out well. And I had fondly imagined, before reading this book, that his educational theories grew out of his experience with us, his children! I found to my chagrin that it was not so. Even in education we made little contribution to his life, except perhaps to demonstrate that theory is easier than practice.

My father had written in this book that "those who are to begin the regeneration of the world must face loneliness, opposition, poverty, obloquy. They must be able to live by truth and love, with a rational unconquerable hope; they must be honest and wise, fearless, and guided by a consistent purpose." To his admirers he seemed to be such a man himself. He had given away his inheritance because he thought it wrong to have such an unfair advantage. He had lost the respect of conventional friends by refusing to perpetuate the hypocrisy of a dead marriage. He had forfeited his comfortable post at Trinity by his opposition to the war. He had struggled ceaselessly for war's victims for four long years, even going to prison himself. He was a man who had "every advantage of wealth and breeding," plus intellectual brilliance and considerable fame—and he put all this at the service of mankind, as he understood its interests. He was a true hero in his public life, and neither praise nor blame could deflect him from what he considered the truth.

This was the man my mother came to know in 1919. Dora Black was a fellow of Girton then, young, beautiful and brilliant, with a promising academic career ahead of her, should she care to pursue it. She was energetic and optimistic, and she had many plans and hopes for a life of her own in a world which began to seem wider and more open than anything she had known in the comfortable home of her civil-servant father. She had first met my father in 1916, through a friend who was one of his pupils, and had astonished him by saying that what she most wanted was to marry and have children—not at all what was expected of intellectual young women in those days. By the time they met again in 1919, through the same friend, she had become a convinced feminist. This time she exasperated my father by asserting that any children she bore would be hers alone and she would not readily recognize the father's rights. "Well, whoever I have children by," he said, "it won't be you!"

My father's old affair with Colette was on again, off again, as exhaustingly up and down as a roller coaster. He was ready to turn to someone new. Besides, Colette had never wanted children, whereas my mother was as eager for them as my father was. She believed strongly that such a great man should perpetuate himself through children, which must have been pleasant for him to hear after his grandmother's old prophecies of doom. Dora herself had had a happy childhood and she felt that raising children was a pleasant and worth-while occupation, provided she could do it on her own terms. The feeling she inspired in my father was quite different from his intense romantic passion for Colette; almost from the start, he wanted my mother to be his wife, and he began to think of divorcing Alys, after almost ten years of separation.

But being a wife was not at all what my mother wanted. "Women who have been free remember the horror of the approach to marriage," she said. "A barrier for most of us to free public activity; a lifelong contract only to be broken in disgrace and public disgust."

"She was a little disappointed," wrote my father, looking back, "to find that almost immediately our relations took on all the character of marriage, and when I told her that I should be glad to get a divorce and marry her, she burst into tears, feeling, I think, that it meant the end of independence and light-heartedness." Feeling also, I imagine, that her unconventional idol had let her down by wanting the legal stability she was so anxious to escape.

My father was a feminist too, of course. His parents had been feminists, his first wife was a feminist, he had campaigned for women's votes long before it was fashionable. But feminism did not mean the same to him as to my mother. He was willing to treat her with absolute respect, grant her every possible privilege, but he wanted her to make being his wife her career, and it was not a career she would have chosen for herself.

Sometimes I think my mother should have been born into a matriarchy, for she has always been convinced that all wisdom resides in mothers and, consequently, all power should be theirs also. All her years of feminist activity were devoted to improving the lot of mothers, fighting for their right to health care, to birth-control information, to control of the money they needed for their children. She has always seen the family more as a biological unit of mother and young than as a unit of society headed by a breadwinning male, and she communicated this attitude to both her daughters, as well as to the girls in her school. We grew up with a passionate pride in our ability to grow a child, convinced that we could do anything a man could do plus this other, and were thus truly superior people. For this I am profoundly grateful to my mother.

My mother always felt that a woman who rejected motherhood for reasons of convenience or appearance or pleasure would find herself condemned to a life of barren selfishness. Even women who gave up children for careers were probably mistaken, though it was not their fault; she blamed masculine society for forcing such a choice upon them. And upon her. She loved my father very much and admired him also. It must have been flattering, too, to have such a famous man so passionately anxious to marry her. But was it worth the price? When her first book came out as by "Mrs. Bertrand Russell" and was mistakenly listed in some library catalogues as by him, she truly felt the cost. She had ceased to be a person and had become a wife. No wonder she resisted so long. I sometimes think it was only to legitimize John, a matter of profound importance to my father, that she did in the end agree to marry him.

But before then they had lived through much together and had traveled half over the world.

As a radical, my father had been much excited by the Russian Revolution and he was anxious to go and see for himself what the Bolsheviks were really doing. His opportunity came in 1920, when he was invited to accompany a Labour deputation and the Russians agreed to admit him. My mother, who was anxious to see Russia too, wanted to go with him, but he refused.

"No," he said. "Typhus is raging in Russia and it's not at all safe. Besides, you've never been interested in politics, so why should you go?"

And off he went, expecting her to stay put till he got back.

That is the story he tells in his *Autobiography*. My mother's version is rather different. They do not seem ever to have agreed on anything to do with Russia—in fact, they quarreled bitterly about going to Russia, they quarreled about Russia itself, they quarreled in retrospect about the circumstances of the trip. They went on quarreling about Russia for years.

In 1920 it was almost impossible to get into Russia except as part of some official delegation. The borders were sealed from within and without, the place was blockaded, all foreigners were suspect, hunger, disease and fighting were widespread. But my mother was determined to see for herself. She set out for Scandinavia on her own and, after a series of mysterious contacts and adventurous journeys, succeeded in getting into Russia in a small boat.

Once there, she became aware, like my father, of the atmosphere of suspicion and mistrust. You could not speak freely. Anyone might be a secret Soviet agent or the disguised tool of reaction; one would denounce you on the spot, the other after you got home, and some worked for both sides at once and would sell you to the highest bidder. This was unpleasant, but she saw good things there too. She saw hope for the future and plans for equality, she met men she admired, and she acquired a deep love for the Russian people that lasted all her life, too often predisposing her to believe their propaganda and take their hopes for facts.

When my father got out of Russia, heartsick over the suffering he had seen and the cynical cruelty of the Bolsheviks, Dora was nowhere to be found. Almost by chance he discovered that she had gone to Russia on her own and was still there. Frantic but helpless, he could do nothing but wait, like a woman, for the return of the beloved from distant adventures. When he began getting smuggled letters from her, which indicated that she liked the dreadful place, his astonishment and his anger knew no bounds. Grieved over the misery he had seen and distressed by my mother's actions, he returned to Colette for comfort. He must have felt, at that point, that there was nothing to hope for from my mother. "I wondered," he said, "whether we should ever be able to overcome this difference" over Russia.

Nevertheless, when he found he had been invited to China to lecture for a year, "I decided I would accept if Dora would come with me, but not otherwise." He contrived to get a message to her in Russia, she managed to get out of the country and come home, and they began at once to quarrel about Russia while all the time preparing to set out for a year in China together.

It was the beginning of a remarkable partnership. He was an urbane man of the world, much traveled and highly sophisticated; an aristocrat, a brilliant philosopher and a famous man; though he probably didn't realize it, he automatically expected a certain amount of deference and respect. And he was almost old enough to be her father. My mother, still young, loved and admired him deeply, but she was never a docile worshiper. She expected to be a partner in his work, not an auxiliary to her husband's career. My father told a friend once that "living with her was as relaxing as travelling on an express train bearing one to one's destination without effort on one's part." She always had enough energy for two. This was all right as long as they agreed on the destination, but hopeless once they began going in different directions.

They arrived in China confident of their love, yet uncomfortably conscious of their profound differences of opinion. There they found themselves at once in an environment so much more foreign than anything they had known before that they inevitably became more aware of what they had in common than of what divided them. One could not even enter a house in China without coming face to face with strangeness, for one had to zigzag past a series of walls built to keep out demons, who could travel only in straight lines.

They liked China at once, captivated by the beauty of the countryside and its buildings and charmed by the elegance of Chinese furniture and ornaments. As soon as they had a house of their own, they furnished it with Chinese things, to the regret of the progressive Chinese who had invited them, to whom these lovely things were symbols of a reactionary past. My father agreed with them in theory, but he rather regretted it, for old Chinese things were very beautiful and many of the old customs he found most congenial. The calm good manners of the Chinese, their belief in moderation and self-control, impressed him, as did the respect they accorded to learning. He was enchanted by their subtle and pervasive humor and found the cultured Chinese very much his kind of people. Indeed, if he had been able to eliminate his red face, his deafening laugh and his European vigor, he could easily have passed for a Chinese sage.

I was not born until three years after the Chinese visit, and all I have to say about it is conjecture and hearsay. It comes into my story as the foundation of our family life and the source of much of our family folklore. To this day, when I think of my father I see him in an armchair on a Chinese rug, his Chinese paintings hanging behind him and his Chinese ornaments on the mantelpiece beside him. He and my mother brought home rugs and hangings, furniture, paintings and ornaments, which furnished every house I can remember living in. The things they brought home were lovely enough to give pleasure to anyone who looked at them, and for my parents they had the added pleasure of nostalgic associations; while for me, as a child, they were exciting as well as lovely, endowed with magic properties. Many of them were delicate carvings in ivory, which we were allowed to touch only with the greatest care and reverence, confirming my belief in their special power. I regarded them as talismans of happiness and believed that, if I only knew the spell, they would bring me the joy they had once obviously brought my parents.

There was one spell that John and I knew and often used to conjure up family happiness and establish an atmosphere of cheerful reminiscence. The magic words were "Tell me about China, Daddy," and they almost never failed.

Living in China had been such a romantic experience for our parents that even the act of recalling it for us, their children, seemed to have power to bring them together again. China, I think, was one of the few things on which they did not disagree. John used to use the magic spell rather wickedly to postpone the moment of bedtime, knowing that his father's passion for imparting knowledge would outweigh his devotion to the stern necessity of adequate sleep. He showed us maps and pictures of the places he had been; he told us about the Great Wall of China and about Marco Polo, making it seem like a fairy tale, and he recounted stories about the funny things that had happened while he and my mother were there. My favorite was always the one about the very beginning of the visit. He had been invited to China by someone called Fu Ling Yu and had wondered idly whether it was some kind of practical joke. However, when his fare and my mother's were paid, he concluded that nobody would indulge in such an expensive joke, and they set out confidently. They arrived in Shanghai, at the end of the long, long journey, only to find that there was no one to meet them! They looked at each other and wondered.

"Fu Ling Yu?" they said to each other apprehensively.

Luckily, it was only a muddle about the time of arrival and they were soon in capable hands.

They lived happily together in China until my father caught pneumonia and nearly died. He always spoke of it jokingly, making light of the suffering and emphasizing the comic aspects, so that I never realized until I read his *Autobiography* how serious it had been.

"My temperature went up to 107 degrees," he would tell us. "Most people die when their fever goes as high as that." This made us feel that he was remarkably tough, and we were proud of him. The horrors of his pneumonia seemed to us more a proof of his endurance than a tale of

woe. Indeed, I always felt that his survival was a demonstration of his skill and strength on a par with scaling a
famous mountain peak. Perhaps he felt that way himself.
He tells in his *Autobiography* how desperately ill he was
and how long it took him to recover, but he sounds quite
cheerful about it, quite pleased with himself, perhaps because he learned something from the experience that made
the suffering worth while. "Lying in my bed feeling that I
was not going to die was surprisingly delightful," he said.
"I had always imagined until then that I was fundamentally
pessimistic and did not greatly value being alive. I discovered that in this I had been completely mistaken, and that
life was infinitely sweet to me."

It was a different experience for my mother, who sat
by his bed alone and far from home, through days and
nights of delirium, watching him struggle for life. All the
anxiety was hers, the loneliness and grief. She must have
lived through a nightmare. He remained frail and subject
to infection for many months afterward, so she had to
watch over him carefully, making sure he took no risks
with his fragile health. Well after they got back to England,
in November, when John was due to be born, my father was
still weak enough for the doctors to fear that any complications in the birth might set off a sympathetic illness in him.
They therefore thought it wise to induce the baby early,
which was supposed to be safer. As a consequence, John
was born with a dislocated jaw, which gave him a bleak
view of life from the beginning.

For my mother and father, the long and tedious period
of his convalescence was made bearable by her discovery
that John was on the way. They were delighted, and I can
picture them together, each tenderly caring for the other's
health for the sake of the coming child they so much desired. As they sat together on the deck of the ship on the
long voyage home, they dreamed magnificent dreams of

the wonderful world their children would create. It did not matter to them at all that most of the passengers, aware of my mother's indecent condition, refused to speak to them. These foolish passengers belonged to the past; their day was over and they could do little harm. The future was with my parents and their unborn children.

"A Generation Educated in Fearless Freedom"

My brother, John, was born in November 1921. When he was almost fifty years old and ready to give up hope of children, my father had a son at last, an heir to the Russell past and a promise for the world's future.

"If existing knowledge were used and tested methods applied, we could, in a generation, produce a population almost wholly free from disease, malevolence and stupidity," he wrote in his enthusiasm. "One generation of fearless women could transform the world by bringing into it a generation of fearless children, not contorted into unnatural shapes, but straight and candid, generous, affectionate, and free. Their ardour would sweep away the cruelty and pain which we endure because we are lazy, cowardly, hard-hearted, and stupid."

My mother was one of these fearless women. For her, the main necessity was to liberate the child from the shackles of his past; after that you could rely on his natural good sense to lead him into the right channels. Her belief was so strong that she often longed to snatch unfortunate children away from their besotted parents and place them in a more suitable environment before they were ruined for life.

Their hopes for their children were almost boundless. "A generation educated in fearless freedom will have wider and bolder hopes than are possible to us, who still have to struggle with the superstitious fears that lie in wait for us below the level of consciousness. Not we, but the free men and women whom we shall create, must see the new world, first in their hopes, and then at last in the full splendor of reality." So wrote my father. "The way is clear," he went on. "Do we love our children enough to take it?" The clear way was that of love informed by modern knowledge. In my mother's words, "those people who are not prepared to equip themselves in the necessary way must either abandon parenthood or have recourse to the expert." The parents who sent their children to board at our school when they were only three or four years old presumably shared this point of view.

John and I were fortunate that our parents were the experts to whom others came; less fortunate in the type of modern knowledge they acquired, that early behaviorism whose clockwork efficiency embittered the infancy of so many of my generation. My father came to think later that the methods he had proposed for very young children were "unduly harsh," but he changed his mind too late to do us any good. At the time, under the spell of scientific optimism, he accepted, applied and expounded an unpleasantly crude kind of conditioning process.

"The right moment to begin the requisite moral training" of children "is the moment of birth, because then it can be begun without disappointing expectations." Parents must begin teaching the child with its very first breath that it has entered into a moral world, in which it will always get its just deserts but must never ask for more. "Infants," my father said, "are far more cunning than grown-up people are apt to suppose; if they find that crying produces agreeable results, they will cry." If a child cries "when there is no adequate physical cause, it must be left to cry; if not, it will quickly develop into a tyrant. When it is attended to, there should not be too much fuss: what is necessary must be done, but without excessive expressions of sympathy."

When my father was three days old, his old-fashioned, sentimental mother wrote of him: "I have lots of milk now, but if he does not get it at once or has wind or anything he gets into such a rage and screams and kicks and trembles till he is soothed off." I wish he could have written about us in the same way. I do not like to think of myself being treated with such austere benevolence, as raw material to be shaped rather than a person to be enjoyed.

"Some of these precepts may seem harsh," he might reply, "but experience shows that they make for the child's health and happiness."

Whose experience? Not mine, either as infant or as mother. When a child is left to cry, it will stop sooner or later, finding it useless, but who can tell what passes in its infant brain? I can remember lying silent behind the bars of my crib at naptime, filled with jealous rage, knowing that John and my father were walking in the sun outside. And when I had infants of my own and saw them thrashing their arms and legs, roaring with crimson desperation, no amount of theory could make me stand by and let them do it.

"We should not give the child a sense of self-importance which later experience will mortify, and which, in any case, is not in accordance with the facts," wrote my father, and he repeated the same advice many times in different words. When I read it recently, I was hurt to think I had spent my infancy in such an atmosphere of antiseptic affection, even though I understood that what he "meant" was that those whom the child loves may die and leave it comfortless (as he himself had been left), and therefore it is best that the child should learn from birth to rely on no one but itself.

My father's respect for science, coupled with his rejection of all old-fashioned orthodoxy, led him into absurdities that a greater confidence in his own good sense might have avoided. He explained in his book *Education and the Social Order* that when a baby cries, somebody comes to relieve its pain, and so it learns to associate crying with pleasant consequences. Soon it begins to cry "because it desires a pleasure, not because it feels a physical pain," he wrote. "This is one of its first triumphs of intelligence. But try as it may, it cannot give quite the same cry as when it is in actual pain. The attentive ear of the mother knows the difference, and if she is wise she will ignore the cry that is not an expression of physical pain." One might think that an intellectual like my father would be eager to reward the infant's exercise of intelligence, in order to encourage it to go on thinking. One might think also that he would want the child to feel that desiring pleasure is normal among human beings and sometimes leads to its attainment. But he was mesmerized by the authorities, who insisted that regularity and sleep were more essential to the child's well-being than anything else.

I wonder if he ever learned to distinguish between the cry of pain and the cry of mental distress, or if he thought that only mothers could attain that sensitive skill. I never did myself.

From a very early age, John and I were aware that our father was famous and admired. From his conversation and our mother's, we knew that they were enlightened parents and that it was a privilege to belong to their family; they knew what was best for their children and did not repeat blindly the mistakes of their own upbringing. Consequently, we need never feel afraid, we could speak to our parents about anything, we were free and healthy and privileged. If we still felt fear, envy, anger, if we were slow to learn and shy to speak, the fault must be in ourselves, since the method was foolproof and the parents were perfect. Or so I thought.

I doubt if my father ever believed in behaviorism quite as thoroughly as he appears to in his book on education; he was far too much the passionate moralist. He may have thought that the right conditioning of his children would produce the right kind of people, but he certainly didn't consider himself the inevitable result of his own conditioning. If my father's view of the inescapable, dreadful results of old-fashioned education had been correct, it would have been quite impossible for him and my mother to be the courageous innovators they undoubtedly were.

"The secret of modern moral education," my father wrote, "is to produce results by means of good habits which were formerly produced (or attempted) by self-control and will-power." In other words, our parents deserved credit for their good behavior, which was the result of intense moral effort, whereas John's and my conditioned virtue was as natural as breathing. Most of the time we were good children, an apparent demonstration of the success of the method, but we knew that it was nowhere near as easy as breathing. It took a great deal of old-fashioned will power, and our failures caused us much unhappiness.

Perhaps that was not too important to my father. Once, when I was reading a life of Shelley, I commented to him that I would rather have my children (if I ever had any) happy than as great as Shelley at the cost of equivalent suffering. He was shocked; Shelley was one of his favorite poets, a hero of his youth, and, besides, mere happiness was never his ambition for his children. He valued intelligence and virtue far above happiness and he always had society in mind as well as the individual. If he could raise children who would devote their lives to relieving the ills of society, that would be a success.

This is an oversimplification. Of course our parents were concerned with the happiness of their children and

did all they could to ensure it; we were not simply means
to an end. But we were not to be happy just for the sake
of being happy; they believed there were moral advantages
to happiness. "Happiness in children is absolutely necessary
to the production of the best kind of human being," said
my father.

My father was a philosopher and a theoretician. He
loved to take a complex problem, reduce it to simple com-
ponents, then show how the parts could be reassembled
into a constructive solution, much as one sorts the jumbled
pieces of a jigsaw puzzle and puts them together to form a
picture. He tackled the education of his children in this
way. Having studied the problem and developed a theory,
he endeavored to put it into practice, apparently believing
that a parent could always behave correctly in the presence
of his children and conceal from them any undesirable
feelings he might possess. If he had had full-time care of
us, he might have been less confident.

Or if he had paid a little more attention to the theories of Freud and less to those of the American behaviorist
John B. Watson. He never realized how much he was
transmitting to us beyond the enlightened theories of his
conscious mind. When my father was a young man, his
grandmother had written to him about his childhood: "You
would always cheerfully give up your own wishes for those
of others, never attempt an excuse when you had done
wrong, and never fail to receive warning or reproof as gratefully as praise." I cannot think it was part of his plan to
pass on this attitude to me, yet he succeeded admirably in
doing so.

In order to be the "splendid human beings" our parents hoped for, John and I had need of great courage,
to be instilled in us by the moral training of our early childhood. Our parents hoped, in fact, to do much more than
give us the old-fashioned kind of courage, which was based
on concealment of fear; they hoped to train us to feel no

fear at all, except what my father called "the rational apprehension of danger." (Ordinary courage was unsatisfactory, because repressed fears can emerge from the unconscious transformed into impulses of cruelty.) Consequently, they devoted much time and thought to training in courage, and my father wrote a long chapter, in his book on education, describing their method and its apparent success. In that chapter he cited an experiment by Dr. J. B. Watson in which that great scientist taught a child to be afraid of rats "by repeatedly sounding a gong behind its head at the moment when he showed it a rat. The noise was terrifying, and the rat came to be so by association." Although my father never went so far as to experiment on us in this way, it was with the same disapassionate scientific attitude that he set out to observe John's childish anxieties. Reading his account much later, I was belatedly thankful that I had been too young to participate fully in the experiment.

When John was nearly two years old, he had a new nurse, who was "generally timid and especially afraid of the dark. He quickly acquired her terrors . . . and was even afraid of his little sister the first time he saw her. . . . All these fears," my father wrote, "might have been acquired from the timid nurse; in fact they gradually faded away after she was gone." It is just possible that they derived from loss of an old nurse combined with the departure of his mother to have a new baby, but that goes too deep for my father's theory. In his view, fears were either instinctive or learned, whether from example or from unpleasant experience. He did not regard them as manifestations of psychological distress unable to express itself in other ways. It was as though the child had no internal life of its own, only an external surface to be molded according to the parent's desire.

John was also irrationally frightened by moving shadows and mechanical toys "which no grown-up person would find alarming." These were dealt with by reasoning, by scientific demonstration of their groundlessness and by gradual familiarization with the feared object. "In no case did we entirely remove the terrifying object: we put it at a distance . . . and we persisted till the fear completely ceased. . . . I think an irrational fear should never be simply let alone, but should be gradually overcome by familiarity with its fainter forms." This strikes me as a little like keeping a small pebble in one's shoe, in the hope of gradually learning to walk with a large stone. Why not simply remove it?

I have talked so far about the little fears that children suffer, distressing while they last but usually soon outgrown, no matter how they are treated. The immense and terrible anxieties of childhood, unconquerable without adult help, are a more difficult proposition. What did my father do about John's fear of the dark?

"One night there was a terrific gale, and a hurdle was blown over with a deafening crash. He woke in terror, and cried out. I went to him at once: he had apparently waked with a nightmare, and clung to me with his heart beating wildly. Very soon his terror ceased. But he had complained that it was dark . . . so I gave him a night-light. After that, he made an almost nightly practice of crying out, until at last it became clear that he was only doing it for the pleasure of having grown-up people come and make a fuss. So we talked to him very carefully about the absence of danger in the dark, and told him that if he woke he was to turn over and go to sleep again, as we should not come to him unless there was something serious the matter. He listened attentively, and never cried out again except for grave cause on rare occasions. Of course the night-light was discontinued. If we had been more indulgent, we should probably have made him sleep badly for a long time, perhaps for life."

Dear, good John! He never cried out again except on

rare occasions, but he did not lose his fears. He knew that the dark was not dangerous in the way that lions and tigers and cliffs were dangerous; I am sure he understood in the marrow of his bones the difference between "rational apprehension" of real danger and the panic terrors of the night. But both kinds were real to him, and his fear did not vanish because his father told him it was irrational. "Of course the night-light was discontinued," and of course he never cried out again as he lay alone in the dark. Behaviorist method triumphed and good sleeping habits were assured. But the fears remained. They grew and grew and grew, secretly, in John as in me, festering quietly and sapping our vitality.

My father used to tell us a story about a long-ago emperor of China whose courtiers wished, for some reason, to get rid of him. They decided to drive him mad and set about doing so with typical Chinese subtlety. One day, when the emperor was reviewing a magnificent procession of knights and nobles on the grandest and fieriest steeds, he observed one warrior in the midst of the procession riding on a camel.

"What is that man doing on a camel?" he asked.

"Camel, your majesty?" they replied. "Camel? We don't see any camel."

Next day, at a feast, a man appeared in rags.

"What is that man doing in rags?" asked the emperor.

"Man in rags, your majesty?" the courtiers said. "We see no man in rags."

And so they went on, day after day, till the poor man thought he must be mad and decided to abdicate.

So it was with our fears.

In Cornwall, the bitter cold Atlantic roars up onto the sand, sweeping uninterrupted all the way from Nantucket. There are days when even the hardiest swimmer will not venture in, and many grownups have been known to quail before the Cornish breakers. I remember an American visitor one summer, parent of one of the children in the school, I think, who went down to the beach alone. When he returned we asked if he had gone swimming.

"No," he replied. "I had intended to enter the water, but the billows were too considerable."

This wild, cold ocean was John's introduction to the water, and he found it frightening, to the distress of his parents, who set to work to cure him of his fears. They put him into shallow tidal pools until he got used to the cold; they let him play on the sand within hearing of the noise of the waves, though out of sight; then they took him to watch the waves and "made him notice that after coming in they go out again." This was the summer when John was two and a half years old and I was six months.

Next year, when he was three and a half, John was still afraid of the water, and his enlightened parents lost patience with him. "We adopted old-fashioned methods. When he showed cowardice, we made him feel that we were ashamed of him; when he showed courage, we praised him warmly. Every day for about a fortnight, we plunged him up to the neck in the sea, in spite of his struggles and cries. Every day they grew less; before they ceased, he began to ask to be put in. . . . Fear had not ceased altogether, but had been partly repressed by pride."

It was not easy to please them. My father used to tell with amusement of my childish effort to write John's name upon the sand when I was perhaps two years old. Having succeeded in this stupendous achievement, I fetched him to admire the result.

"Yes, that's very nice, Kate," he said. "Very nice indeed. But, you know, we usually write the *J* the other way round."

He was such a kind man, my father, yet his method of education seems full of brutal assaults on the childish mind. Had he quite forgotten how a child feels?

In my father's memory, "it was always sunny, and

always warm after April" in Cornwall, sunny and warm and peaceful and happy, all discord eliminated by reason and right methods. That was the Garden of Eden. I used to think that only his sunny reality was true; the darkness of rain and storm and fury existed only in my mind. I know now that both were real; I have known it for a long time, but I never tried to tell him. I was afraid to, feeling sure he would convince me my perception was wrong, thus confusing me even further. Or, worse, I might have convinced *him* and then, seeing that all was not good, he would have thought it all bad and been profoundly unhappy. In fact, he came to think that anyway. "Having failed as a parent . . ." he says in his *Autobiography*, at the end of his account of his second marriage. Failed because the rosy dreams of the early years had proved a delusion, and it was all much more difficult and complex than he had imagined.

I did not want to add to his sense of failure. Of course he wasn't a failure as a parent; I owe him almost all that is good in me. But he wasn't a hundred-per-cent success either, and I couldn't have told him that without his hearing "failure." So I didn't tell him. And we *had* had a real Garden of Eden, even though the snake had been there all the time.

Beacon Hill School

In the Biblical story of the Garden of Eden, Adam and Eve lost their innocent joy when they accepted the snake's offer of knowledge, which was to make them like gods. When our parents established Beacon Hill School, in 1927, John and I began a similar exchange, though the circumstances were less dramatic. During our years at that school, we lost our childhood happiness and received in return a fantastic education. That had not been the intention of the school; indeed, our parents founded it partially because they were unwilling to purchase our education at the expense of our happiness, as so many parents did and still do. At the same time, they were reluctant to preserve our innocent bliss at the expense of our acquisition of knowledge, as they saw many progressive schools doing. They saw no solution but to start a new school of their own, where we could be educated as they thought proper.

Just as they began looking for a large country house in which to establish the school, my father's brother found himself forced by lack of money to give up his house. With great reluctance, for he loved the place, he rented it to my father for the school, and we went to live on Beacon

Hill, among the South Downs, about sixty miles from London. Uncle Frank's house was called Telegraph House,
because it had been one of a string of hilltop heliograph
stations that flashed messages from Portsmouth to London
in the time of George III. My father used to say that perhaps the news of Trafalgar had reached London by way of
Telegraph House. The house itself was ugly and inefficient
and absurd; it seemed to have spread over the ground
without any kind of plan. Among its oddities was an odd
square tower with a room at the top whose four large windows looked north, south, east and west, over the fields
and woods for miles around, to a silver line of sea on the
horizon: Southampton, where the ships for America came
and went.

My father made this tower room his study and dec-
orated it with many of the beautiful things he had brought
back from China. There he sat and wrote, surrounded by
his bronze and ivory treasures and the wide view he loved,
with a telescope for the entertainment and instruction of
the young. He gave us history lessons up there, during
which we would sit on the soft blue-and-white rug in front
of the fire and listen with fascination to his vivid accounts
of ancient episodes. He was like a tower himself, taking us
up and opening windows for us onto a vast world whose
existence we had never even imagined. You could ask him
about Alexander or Charlemagne or Henry VIII, and he
would say, "Well, it was like this . . ." and launch into a
long and lively account. I took it for granted, living with
him, that adults were like that, and that I would be like
that too when I grew up.

Not long ago I received a letter from an old family
friend who worked for many years at the school, recalling
the magnetic power of that tower study. "You used to
wander up those stairs to his tower room. Nobody could
ever find you, there you were looking through a telescope

for miles and miles. Then BR would bring you down to whoever's class you were in. And of course I remember the history classes BR used to take and everybody loved them. How they all used to run up those stairs!"

It was an ideal place for a free school. Around the house there stood some two hundred acres of private woods, where we could safely roam at will, and beyond that lay miles and miles of downland, smooth grassy hills of chalk to be run up and rolled down and walked over and explored ad infinitum. The nearest villages were almost three miles away, the nearest house a mile, the nearest town ten miles. Here we could be really free, eccentric as we pleased in dress and manners, without fear of observation from curious and disapproving neighbors. Of course the school was news, both for its own sake and for my father's, and a steady stream of visitors and journalists from London came down to look and listen, take pictures and interview my parents. A time-consuming nuisance for the adults, no doubt, but they never bothered us children much—not as much as we bothered them.

The story was told of our school, as of all other progressive schools, about the journalist who rang the bell at the front door and was startled to have it opened by a naked child.

"Oh my God!" the journalist exclaimed.

"He doesn't exist," the child replied, and shut the door.

We treated this story with the contempt it deserved because we knew we didn't have a front doorbell. However, our isolation protected us from such encounters and allowed us to work out our own ways of living, without interference. We did not know we were odd; we thought we were enlightened and wise and superior to others, living a better life. Many years later, I took my husband, a very reasonable young man, to visit Dartington Hall

School, which had always seemed to me most respectable compared to Beacon Hill. When I saw how flabbergasted he was by the shabby untidiness of the children, I got a new perspective on my childhood. We were freaks and never knew it, because we lived protected from the world.

After my parents separated, my mother kept the school going and my father had no more contact with it, which led some people to suppose that the school had been more her idea than his, something in which he had merely acquiesced to please her. This is a misinterpretation of events. He says in his *Autobiography*: "Dora and I came to a decision, for which we were equally responsible, to found a school of our own in order that our children might be educated as we thought best"; and I see no reason to doubt his words.

Because my father was a very polite man, a peaceable man and a diffident Russell, he may have seemed to people to be under his wives' thumb (or thumbs). Sometimes I have thought so myself. Certainly he let his wives, each in turn, determine the atmosphere of his home and even many of his activities, more than is common among men. Often his wives collaborated in his work, which then necessarily took on some of their character—though usually less than they themselves desired. But was this because he was henpecked or because he respected the rights of women and the intelligence of his wives?

His thoughts were always his own, and his essential personal habits, such as tea and tobacco, survived through every transformation of his surroundings. Yet I can see how his changing exterior might mislead people. I have no personal knowledge of his first marriage, of course, but to judge from letters and photographs he was then upright, austere and passionately moral. With my mother, he was jolly, rather fat, more than a bit shabby and always ready to outrage conventional sensibilities. In my stepmother's beautiful house, he was well dressed, sharply witty, urbane and not, I think, very happy. I do not know much about his life with his fourth wife, Edith, except that he was happy in it and charmingly ready to entertain visitors with brilliant reminiscence.

But these are personal matters. In the field of ideas and public action he was always his own master, not to be intimidated by anybody. Without the energy and confidence of my mother, he might not have had the determination to start a school—after all, neither of them knew anything about running a school—but neither would he have had the children to start it for. They both believed equally in the school at the beginning, they both worked just as hard at it, and each hoped for identical wonderful results from it.

The children in the school were to have absolute freedom of inquiry; our natural curiosity was to be encouraged in every way and all our questions answered as truthfully as possible. It was hoped that, in this way, we would acquire an interest in learning and a habit of seeking after truth. The teaching was to be based on our appetite for knowledge, rather than on a preconceived program of basic skills and facts to be fed into the living computer of each child's mind.

We were not left entirely free, however. My parents believed that a good deal of scientific supervision was necessary to ensure the production of the healthy, well-educated and self-disciplined adults they desired. They never imagined that undirected children would eat what they should, sleep when they should, learn all that they needed to know. But they believed that children would be more likely to acquire proper mental and physical habits through adult encouragement than through adult command; and they wanted us to do the right thing because we understood its rightness, not because we were compelled to do it. We were expected to rule ourselves, under the wise supervision of benevolent adults, and to learn very quickly to behave well even when we were not watched, an expectation that made the moral climate remarkably bracing. We could never be irresponsibly lazy or malicious and trust to the teachers to control the consequences of our behavior. Whatever we did we had to live with, and our actions were liable to be very critically discussed at school-council meetings, which included all the children and all the teachers, each with one vote.

The school council made all the rules for the school except in matters of health. Since children outnumbered teachers, we could have outvoted them at any time had we wanted to—a nightmare situation for nervous administrators. In practice, we were heavily outweighed in wisdom and experience by the teachers, and we knew it. We debated with heat and abandon, but usually we accepted the recommendations of their superior wisdom. Except once, when we voted to abolish *all* rules for a trial period, to discover which ones were really important. I doubt if the teachers were comfortable with that experiment, but it proved a good one, because we were not comfortable either. The teachers took the line that rules were abolished for them too, and the consequence was such dreadful anarchy that we were all thankful to return to the rule of law.

The first thing that comes to mind when I recall the school is the front hall, a large L-shaped room with dark paneled walls and parquet floor, many doors and a wide oak staircase behind ornamental wooden pillars. One arm of the L, bright and sunny and warmed by radiators, was used as the children's dining room and was full of small tables and chairs. I remember this hall as a place of desolation. I remember standing in the middle of the polished floor, surrounded by space and dark woodwork, not knowing which way to go or what to do, having no belonging place in all that vast building. This must be a memory from the very beginning of the school, when we were all new there, for I spent seven years at Beacon Hill and came to know it intimately, inside and out. Yet still, when I recall the hall, that desolation is uppermost in my mind.

I remember too walking along the hall at the top of the stairs one day, stepping carefully along the edge of the apple-green carpet and running my hand along the wide oak balustrade above the stairs.

Somebody said: "Happy birthday!"

"Oh, is it my birthday?"

"Yes, you're four years old today."

It must have been the same for all the little children in the school, some of whom came from far away. All the security of home had vanished, and we had to find our own routine, our own identity, our own belonging place, in a vast house full of terrifyingly boisterous children. Maybe many of the homes were bad, benighted, even unloving; but at least they were familiar. Of course we found security soon enough, in the routine of the school and in the rooms we used, but the first shock was chilling. And even after the first, one never felt entirely safe there. In all children's tag games, there is a "base," a place of temporary safety where one can rest unmolested. In the whole of Beacon Hill there was no "base," and without such a refuge we were forlorn at heart, no matter how sturdily independent and bright we seemed. At least I was.

My father wrote, looking back on the school: "For us personally, and for our two children, there were special worries. The other boys naturally thought our boy was unduly favored, whereas we, in order not to favor him or his sister, had to keep an unnatural distance between them and us except during the holidays. They, in turn, suffered from a divided loyalty; they had either to be sneaks or to practice deceit towards their parents. The complete happiness that had existed in our relations to John and Kate was thus destroyed, and was replaced by awkwardness and embarrassment."

I remember feeling this, though I did not clearly realize at the time what was happening. I knew I had no more claim on my parents than any of the other children did, for they were much occupied by the business of running the school, and when they appeared among us we all had to share them equally.

"I can remember," a friend wrote to me recently, "BR walking and walking around Telegraph House holding your hand. You must have been about four years old. Maybe you don't remember, but BR seemed to have so much patience." No, I don't remember, though old school photographs suggest that her memory is better than mine. What I remember is being just one of the children, having no special position and feeling vaguely unhappy about it.

There were also practical reasons for being unhappy. Some of the other children were quite frightening, and there was no one I could go to for protection without being called a telltale, as I often was. My loyalties were so divided and my timidity so great that I may well have been a sneak, even though I thought I was only seeking safety. My best refuge in the early years was a housemaid called Evelyn, who was less compromising as a friend than a teacher would have been and more comforting than one of the children. Yet even her friendship had a price: the mockery of the other children, who jeered and called me "Evelyn's pet."

I was teased off and on all through the years at Beacon Hill, and I teased others in my turn when I felt safe enough, though only in moderation. Poor John, though, was teased unmercifully and incessantly by many of the boys, for he was little and excitable and fun to tease—he was easily brought to the verge of hysterics—and he was a readily available stand-in for his parents, the authorities of the school. I do not see how John endured it as he did; my blood used to boil, just listening, and I would have done anything in the world to stop it.

My father said afterward: "Many of the children were cruel and destructive. To let the children go free was to establish a reign of terror, in which the strong kept the weak trembling and miserable. . . . I found myself, when the children were not at lessons, obliged to supervise them continually to stop cruelty." He had not expected this, and it disappointed him; the apostle of children's liberation found himself playing policeman instead, a role he found exhaustingly uncongenial.

My mother had a thicker skin, perhaps. She had been to an ordinary school with ordinary children and she knew how they behaved. Knowing her, I think it likely that in her own childhood she was one of the strong and had rarely experienced the anguish of the victim. "While nobody would wish to allow a big child to use another brutally," she said, "is it not sounder for children to learn tolerance by their battles with other children, their natural peers, than by adult discipline or the smooth control of 'atmosphere' and communal duties?"

Many of the children at Beacon Hill were problems, sent to us as a last resort, and they vented on others the griefs and frustrations of their private lives. That their cruelty had been learned at home, and was more their misfortune than their fault, afforded little comfort to their victims. The atmosphere of Beacon Hill probably helped them, but they were not particularly good for us. The companionship of other children, which our parents had desired for us, turned out to be a mixed blessing.

Had the machinery of the school been able to run by itself, and my parents been free to devote their attention to the children, as they had intended, the atmosphere might have been different and pleasanter. But they found they had far less time than they had expected for the central task of developing the children's minds and characters. Being without administrative experience, they had been quite unprepared for the amount of time consumed by hiring and overseeing staff, ordering supplies, planning menus, meeting parents and visitors, solving problems, paying bills and collecting fees, and all the rest of it. Besides, the school steadily lost money, so that to keep it going my father had to devote much of his time to popular writing and lecturing.

Freedom at Beacon Hill did not extend to matters of health. My mother wanted all the children in the school to grow up healthy and tough, able to live rough and eat plain, so that they would be adaptable soldiers for reform in a world much in need of change. She offered us her own austere kind of freedom, a freedom from comfort as well as from restrictions.

We had no voice in bedtime. We slept in dormitories, five or six beds to a room, and each of us had a place to keep clothes and private treasures. The beds were comfortable, though the rooms were bare, without rugs or curtains or shades for the light bulbs hanging from the ceiling. I think this bareness was good: less stuff for us to worry about damaging, less clutter to interfere with our living. We always slept with open windows and no more than two blankets, no matter what the weather. I still recall the contortions I went through at night to get my feet warm before thrusting them down to the cold end of the bed, and I remember one awful morning when we woke to find a pile of snow on the cold radiator under the window. We were required to have a cold shower in the morning too, standing in line in the chilly bathroom for the token sprinkling that was all the water supply allowed.

We had no voice in the food, which was dreary institutional English, though eminently nourishing. Although we were officially allowed to leave anything we didn't like, the teachers in charge of the dining room made it difficult for us to do so. We ate together in the children's dining room, waiting in line for our food and sitting wherever we liked at the low tables. For the sake of our teeth, all bread was baked hard in the oven before we ate it and was kept in big tins, which were on the serving tables at every meal. Once in a long while we managed to eat up all the baked bread and ask for more, so that they had to give us ordinary soft bread: a great triumph! There was a rule of either butter or jam, which I always thought was a matter of health, like all the other food rules, though in fact it was only an economy. Cookies were rare, cake unknown, sugar frowned upon unless it was deep dark brown. There were no snacks between meals, and everything was extremely plain and nutritious. We did not always like it, but we felt wiser than those who ruined their teeth and digestion with sweets.

Though we were not free to ruin our health with late hours and bad food, we were never required to "behave ourselves" at meals, which were often quite wild occasions. A favorite amusement was putting a dab of butter on the end of a knife and flicking it at the ceiling, where it stuck and gradually melted away into a grey grease spot.

"Good manners—sitting still, eating tidily, speaking quietly, not hitting, or telling people what you think of them—are a strain we should not ask the very young child to bear. . . . I would prefer the child who waves his spoon while he tells Bill about an airplane to one who is so occupied with etiquette that he forgets what he meant to say." My mother wrote this in her book *In Defence of Children*, she believed it and she acted on it.

For some obscure reason, drinking with meals was supposed to be bad for us. We had to wait until after the meal, when tin mugs of tepid water would appear on large tin trays, to be instantly grabbed by thirsty children. After a particularly dry meal, we would all sit in a row on the bottom step of the stairs, as close as possible to the kitchen door, waiting for the water tray to come in.

Fresh air was considered indispensable. We spent a great deal of time out of doors and went for long walks in all kinds of weather. How well I remember the misery of numb, cold feet inside my boots, the forlorn feeling of seeing the walking group disappear over the next hill as I toiled along the road, the chill of rain trickling down my neck. Perhaps we could have refused to go on these outings, but nobody ever did. We also had outdoor classes and nature study and camp beds for sleeping out. A group of us would carry beds to a suitable spot, wrap ourselves up warmly and lie there contemplating the stars. Then the bugs would come: ants and earwigs crawling up from below, flies and gnats buzzing down from the sky. Then the noises: creakings and rustlings in the bushes, far-off cries of night animals, moaning and muttering of the wind. The darkness was absolute. Clouds swept over the stars and rain fell gently on our blankets. Those brave enough to survive all the other terrors usually gave up at this point and crept back to the house with their blankets.

The fresh-air regime did not seem to bring the glowing good health my parents hoped for. I remember an endless succession of coughs and colds and fevers and tiresome days in bed, not to mention the perennial minor miseries of chapped hands, sore noses and chilblained feet. Winter often found a roomful of us in bed, sitting with our heads under towels inhaling the fragrant steam of Friar's Balsam for colds, gargling with horrible mixtures for sore throats, ventilating thermometers through the corners of our mouths in the hope of bringing them down to normal, which would allow us to get up.

Sometimes there were quite serious illnesses, such as dreadful earaches, endured stoically until the doctor came with her horrible instruments and did something drastic, like piercing the eardrum. We hated the doctor, a pale, red-haired woman, who came periodically even when we were well. When we were ill, her arrival did nothing to cheer us, although her ministrations generally cured us. On her routine visits, we stood along the edge of the drive and shouted at her car as she came and went: "Stinky Dr. Taylor! Stinky Dr. Taylor!" It is a wonder she kept on coming, but perhaps the pay was good.

In the outdoor life of Beacon Hill, there was much to give pleasure to those of us who became tough enough to enjoy it. The wild woods were excellent for hunting and tracking amusements, and they provided a vast open-air lab for the study of animals and plant life, as well as an outdoor gymnasium.

Telegraph House had two driveways, each at least a mile long, one of which was rarely used by cars. We called it "the green drive," because it was largely grass-grown. Down at its far end, we found in the woods a grove of straight young ash trees without branches, which we climbed like ropes. When we got high enough, the trees would bend and deposit us back on the ground—but we had to jump away quickly when we let go, for they flipped upright with speed and the top branches could whip you in the face.

We saw deer in the woods, stoats, foxes and snakes; and rabbit warrens on the hills, great cities of tunnels and mounds inhabited by long ears and flashing tails. We knew where to look for snowdrops in February, for wood anemones and primroses and sweet-smelling violets in spring, for hazelnuts and beechnuts, holly and spindleberries in the fall. We were out to see the swallows return in spring and to hear the cuckoo singing in the sleepy sunshine.

The teachers led a strenuous life. Not only did they

have to know their material and make it interesting enough
for us to learn without compulsion; they also had to accompany us on hikes and supervise our meals and play. And
in their free time, if they had any, there was really nowhere to go and nothing to do except more of the same.
Without a formal structure of authority to back them up,
the teachers had only the strength of their own personal-
ities to rely on in the face of children trained and encouraged to ask constant questions, to accept nothing on mere
adult say-so. Those who survived and succeeded won our
respect and affection; the others departed in shame and
despair.

Sometimes my father went for afternoon walks with
us, and this was always a special treat, because he would
make us a little fire from twigs and dry leaves somewhere
along the way. He was a very skillful fire maker, and he
prided himself on being able to make a fire burn without
paper even in the wettest weather. He was also very careful
to keep the fire small and under control, and to put it out
thoroughly before we went on. Except once. It was a day
when the ground was so soggy with melted snow, every
leaf and twig so sodden, that we were sure not even he
would be able to make a fire burn. He searched at the
roots of thick bushes for dry leaves and tiny twigs, piled
them up carefully and soon had a nice little fire going. It
was a windy day, and he would not have made a fire if
everything had not been so wet. But the wind took hold of
his little fire and fanned it into a big one, and soon fire
swept through the dead gorse and heather. We stood terrified, knowing the fire brigade was three miles away down
the hill in Harting, knowing we would first have to walk
back to the house to call them, knowing that there was no
road to our fire and no water to put it out with. Luckily, it
died down and went out on its own; the house was safe
and no damage was done except for the great black scar

on the hillside, which reminded us all of the day when he thought the fire wouldn't burn.

I have spoken about almost everything in the school except the classes, as though all learning were picked up on walks or at play, without any attempt at formal instruction. But it was never a free school in that sense. My father was himself a very learned man, and he believed that "the good life is one inspired by love and guided by knowledge." Hence, the greater the knowledge, the better the life. For my father, the acquisition of knowledge was a pleasure in itself and an unquestioned good, and he assumed it would be so for all children who had not already suffered miseducation. "The sense of understanding what had been puzzling is exhilarating and delightful," he said. "I remember a sense almost of intoxication when I first read Newton's deduction of Kepler's Second Law from the law of gravitation. Few joys are so pure or so useful as this." Probably few are so rare also, since not all of us have his mental capacity. He, however, did not realize his unusualness and expected all the children in the school to experience this joy, just as he assumed that "every good teacher should be able to give it."

My mother shared my father's belief in the value of knowledge, and both parents wanted us to have as much knowledge as possible, for our own good and humanity's. They hoped to make it possible for us to acquire it without pain, through the encouragement of natural curiosity, but, where curiosity failed, they were prepared to use other inducements, rather than let us remain in ignorance. Here they parted company with other believers in progressive methods, and here they made their particular contribution to education, achieving that combination of freedom and learning that all teachers seek and few ever find.

From this distance, much of the Beacon Hill program looks remarkably traditional. All the standard subjects were taught, each in its own compartment, and the children were expected to study these subjects in classes, largely by means of formal instruction. Conventional people visiting the school were horrified by the disorder, but advocates of truly "free" education were equally shocked by the atmosphere of orderly classroom learning. To be sure, we didn't have to go to classes if we didn't want to, but there wasn't much to do when the others were in class, and the classes were usually interesting. I do not remember ever being bored in class at Beacon Hill. Whatever else may have been difficult or unhappy at Beacon Hill, the time spent in learning was always pure pleasure. Classes were often as exciting as my father had hoped they would be, and they were never ever dull.

Let me begin with the science class. The science lab was set up in one of the summer houses Uncle Frank had built in the woods. The building was long and low, like a garage with windows, and it had been provided, for lab purposes, with workbenches, shelves, sink, Bunsen burner and all kinds of equipment. The teacher was a young Russian called Boris, master of puns to rival Nabokov. He began our science teaching with water, showing us that water wouldn't run uphill—and then proceeding to demonstrate that it would if you only made it come down another hill first. I watched the water rising in the sink from a rubber tube connected to a jar on a shelf and was thrilled to discover the secret of fountains. He showed us how fire needs air, by burning a candle inside a bell jar until it went out; he floated a candle on a cork inside the bell jar and we watched the water level rise. And everything he did, he let us do after him.

He never made us feel that this was low-level elementary stuff. Rather, he was a high priest initiating us into mysteries that would become ever more fascinating as we grew older. It was a privilege to know those facts and to try those experiments, not a chore to memorize the stuff and write up the results in notebooks. Science class was as exciting as a magic show in which one is allowed to discover the secrets and practice the tricks.

Once, at the end of the term, we had a science show for parents, where we each demonstrated something we had learned. I performed an experiment that involved making a tremendous white flare. It gave me a great sense of power to explain it to the watching adults and then set off my formidable but safely controlled firework in front of their astonished eyes. Part of Boris's secret was teaching us to use dangerous materials with care and confidence. We knew the dangers of fire and acids, and we knew how to handle them safely, and this made us very proud. This was exactly what my parents had hoped would happen. I think I have never known a better teacher; everything Boris talked about seemed clear and interesting and easy to remember.

French and German were taught by my mother at Beacon Hill, and she did an excellent job of it. I still recall with pleasure listening to the first Linguaphone record, which announced, in a most portentous deep voice: *"Die FamILie is im WOHnzimmer."* We never tired of having this prize joke repeated while we giggled over its solemnity and did our best to imitate it. There was also a delightful book about a remarkable rat family, whose youngest child, Fritz, was incessantly in trouble.

Arithmetic—even my father thought it was difficult for children to learn while they were young. "I remember weeping bitterly because I could not learn the multiplication table," he wrote. He insisted, however, that arithmetic was necessary for practical reasons and must be learned, even though much of it might be tiresome. The burden could be reduced by spreading it thin and doing it for short stretches of time, but it could not be dodged.

The children in his school were not to be allowed to get away with sentimental approximations to knowledge. He succeeded so well that I remember arithmetic with pleasure as a series of challenging puzzles, even though we used very standard texts. Furthermore, I learned enough to start on algebra by the time I was ten years old.

One Beacon Hill teacher who stands out in my memory is Betty, who taught almost everything. She was not a good-natured playmate like Boris, and most of us were a little frightened of her—her last name was Cross, and we made endless jokes about how well it suited her. But she was a masterly teacher. She covered many subjects, and everything she taught she made us understand. I can see her now, standing at the blackboard with a box of colored chalk, making careful diagrams of our internal organs when we studied anatomy. I remember well the fascination of watching the whole picture appear and the despair that resulted from my attempts to copy it into my notebook.

Besides anatomy, she taught us about plants and animals and insects, and made us aware of all that was going on around us outdoors. We went out to see things, to find things, to observe relationships, then returned to read about what we had seen. She showed us how to use the twenty-six volumes of the *Encyclopaedia Britannica,* which stood in a long blue-and-gold row in one of the shelves of her classroom, and she taught us to write about the things we learned from it. Betty often read poems to us and with us, encouraging us to read them on our own, then asking us which we liked and why. She chose all kinds of poems, and never said: "This is great literature by the famous author so-and-so, who lived from such-and-such to such-and-such. See how well he writes." She simply read, then asked us what we thought. Under her direction, we wrote reams of poetry ourselves, and stories of many kinds, with our own illustrations.

The most valuable thing that Betty did for us was to preside over the composition of the plays acted at the end of every term. These were always our plays, not hers, and we felt that she was there only to write them down for us and to give us advice if we asked for it. I cannot imagine how she accomplished this.

Betty's classroom was warm and sunny, with a bright bay window and a smooth oak window seat over the radiator. The room had been built as a library and was lined with shelves and low cupboards where books and supplies were kept. There, in the afternoons, we wrote our plays, slithering up and down the window seat on either side of Betty or fidgeting on small chairs in front of her low table.

"What shall it be this term?"

"Let's do a cave-man play!"

"No, we've already done that. What about a Greek one?"

"That's too much like the Roman one we did last term. Let's do an Egyptian one and put in all those weird animal-headed gods."

"Yes, why don't we?"

"Yes ... yes ... yes. ..."

So the theme was decided.

"Now what about the story?"

"We ought to have somebody die and go down to the Hall of the Dead for judgment."

After long discussion, we settled on a prince who had made trouble by refusing to believe in the old gods. The high priest demanded that he be killed as a human sacrifice, blaming his blasphemy for the crop failures and diseases that were afflicting the country. The prince was perfectly willing to be sacrificed, because he wanted to prove to himself that the gods of the underworld did not exist. After his death, gruesomely enacted on stage, he arrived in the judgment hall, presided over by Isis and Osiris, to be interrogated by the row of grotesque gods appointed to judge the dead. He gave the proper answers to all their ritual questions—then told them that they were all a pack of lies. They fell flat on their faces, and he went back to the world to tell men what he had seen.

This theme of enlightened youth in conflict with hoary superstition was common in our plays, as it was common in our thoughts, but it was rarely a straightforward conflict of good and evil. In the Egyptian play, for instance, the whole action was apparently engineered by Set, the arch-fiend, who appeared far more powerful than all the other gods. When the young prince rushed off on his mission of enlightenment, Set remained behind to say: "No one man can have the influence of Set. I can win back the people to their old ideas."

To write such a play, we had to find out about the beliefs of ancient Egypt, the names of the gods and people and the kinds of clothes they wore. We used the Book of the Dead, which described the ritual of death and judgment and gave pictures of all the curious gods; then the encyclopaedia, to provide the information we needed to make our costumes and scenery. We sewed the clothes and painted the scenery, learned our parts and rehearsed diligently, until at last we were ready to perform for the parents at the end of the term. We did a play about the Crusades too, one about Japan and about the ancient Greeks, the Romans in Britain, a farce about the French Revolution and a play about British India, with an agitator called Wata Rau who used a Yo-Yo as a peace symbol. Our plays were short and violent and often very strange, but a great deal of learning was involved in their production.

The plays were a form of group therapy as well as learning, though nobody thought of them that way at the time. Those who were going to act in them chose their own characters and, as far as possible, each child made up his part, which Betty wrote down as we went along, though everyone was free to offer suggestions to anyone who seemed at a loss. There was tremendous satisfaction in creating one's own role and putting into it all kinds of secret aspirations one was otherwise ashamed to acknowledge. The boy who played Set, for instance, was able for once to make use of angry feelings that were usually nothing but trouble to him and everybody else. In other plays, he created for himself other versions of the destructive social critic. John usually played the intellectual reformer who thought it would be simple to induce people to live in a more rational way. He was often rather ineffectual and found change more complicated and difficult than he expected. I specialized in silly-mother roles, which I created and acted with zest, expressing at the same time my desire to be "just a mother" and my conviction that such a life was contemptible.

The longest and most ambitious of our plays, written when we were already fairly sophisticated playwrights, was a dramatic struggle with the difficulties of our own time and place. It was our attempt to make sense out of the life that confronted us and to find some kind of hope to hold fast to in a world of war and depression and mechanization. The theme was as old as mankind and as new as every generation: a young man sets out in the world, looking for a career that will give meaning to his life.

"I must choose my work soon," he says. "I'm twenty already, yet I can't seem to fit in anywhere. The world doesn't want me much, I reckon, but all the same I'm wanting to do something. Not just messing about, not just making money. I want to be of use and I want to have some fun out of it too. . . . I can't make up my mind at all. It's absolutely hopeless."

A priest comes to offer him the comfort of belief in God, a poet to recommend the beauties of nature, an aviator to sing the praises of knowledge and progress and flying. A bitter, sullen workman comes to criticize them all, then a factory owner to invite the youth into his business and a farmer to advocate the rewards of farming. A painter drifts in and begins to paint his portrait; a scientist asks him to be a guinea pig in an experiment; a "modern" woman appears, with a fine feminist chip on her shoulder, then a female but sexless scientist and a farmer's wife of incredible silliness who lives only for her children (me).

The young man investigates all the life styles offered and finds them useless: the factory owner is a corrupt bully, in whose factory dangerous machines kill and maim the wretched workers; the farmer is financially ruined and loses his farm, a catastrophe that drives his wife to suicide; the aviator is killed in a flying accident, because the factory owner has sold him a rotten plane; the scientist accidentally injects poison into the poet and kills him. A heavy load of disasters, perhaps, yet not too much unlike real life. In the end, the young man gathers all the remaining characters around him and persuades them to go off with him to found a new city, in which to raise the farmer's children to be better and more helpful people. So far, so good; it sounds like a dramatization of my parents' views of life and their hopes for the future through the school. But in one corner of the stage, on a pile of clouds, sit the ghosts of those who have died during the play, and they have the last word.

"Bloody fools," the workman says.

"They've forgotten heredity . . ." the aviator says. "All those children will be the same as their beastly relations when they grow up."

"People never really change— / Life goes on— / Growing and changing— / Yet never moving."

But nobody can hear them, nobody can learn from their experience. Only the priest seems to catch a murmur of something, somebody talking, that he cannot clearly hear.

Most of us were ten to twelve years old when we wrote this play. We might have been expected to fill our days with learning and with play and to leave such adult worries for later. But we were serious people, we thought earnestly about the problems of the modern world, and in our play we took up one by one the solutions offered by different kinds of people.

"If you'd only believe in God, you could never be hopeless."

"Why do you worry about God and the future? It doesn't matter to me who made this daisy, so long as I enjoy its presence. Watch the beauty of the world, love all, then you will need no God but Nature."

"We need accurate knowledge about physics, mechanics, engineering and a dozen other subjects. . . . Life nowadays is impossible without knowledge."

"It's about time you *was* something, sonny. When I was your age I was earning all right."

"I want factories where there are no accidents . . . shorter hours . . . more joy. . . ." "Well, you won't get it —you can't make money that way!"

"Try to realize that all women are not second-rate men, but are a separate class with a definite use in the world beyond mere reproduction."

"Science can alter the world."

"Life should be different," the youth says, after seeing the ruin of all his advisers. "I want to go and arrange things, and make everything fair and pleasant for everyone."

We were pretty sure he couldn't do it, but I think we considered it right for him to devote his life to the attempt. The youth in the play was John, acting out his obligation to realize his father's reforms but expressing by his physical frailness and his hesitancy his uncertainty as to their possibility. Who, after all, was going to help him build the new Jerusalem? The scientist was a ruthless maniac indifferent to human life, the businessman a greedy brute, the farmer a fool, the feminists too obsessed with their own position, the others unable even to survive. Besides the young man himself, only the priest seemed decently kind, yet his kindness was only for individuals, since he did not believe that God's world needed reforming. (It was, incidentally, most unusual for a priest to appear in a sympathetic role in any Beacon Hill production. Generally he was both a fool and a hypocrite.) The message of the play as summed up in the final chorus—"Life goes on— / Growing and changing— / Yet never moving"—is remarkably pessimistic, considering the hopes with which we were surrounded.

My father's scientific optimism was strong and he hoped that we would share it, together with his dispassionate ability to see both sides of a question. But these things are not easy to combine; fair-mindedness puzzled our wills and muddled our hopes, and left us unable to strike out boldly against any enemy, public or private. For it was always possible the enemy was right. My father dealt with this problem by a sort of intellectual conjuring trick: when he wanted to be indignant over evil, he temporarily put away objectivity in some other compartment of his mind. We never managed to learn the trick, and I think he was a little disappointed by our hesitations, not realizing that he had taught them to us himself.

Every self-respecting school has to provide for the arts as well as the more academic subjects. At Beacon Hill we had singing lessons, which were fun, and piano lessons, which varied with the teacher. I loved the piano at first, until we got a strict and academic teacher, who tried to make me learn about theory when I only wanted to play tunes. Besides singing and piano, we had dance lessons. Perhaps "lessons" is not the right word. Out on the green tennis court, surrounded by tall beech hedges, without clothes if the weather was at all warm, we leaped and twisted, twirled and bent, in response to different kinds of music from the old school gramophone and a supply of scratchy, more or less classical records, which sounded quite good out of doors. The one blemish on the pure pleasure of dance classes was the thistles; in the midst of a series of wild Russian leaps across the grass, one might come down on a vicious thistle, which effectively broke up the performance.

Equally happy were our art classes, housed in another of Uncle Frank's odd structures. This one was a long corrugated-iron shed, where nothing could be damaged by paint or water or plaster dust or knives. It was far away from the house and kept all its mess to itself, and it provided many kinds of artistic pleasure. We painted huge pictures on the walls and small ones on paper; we worked with clay and with plaster of Paris; we made potato cuts, printing them on cloth for cushion covers and on paper for decoration; we made elaborate linoleum blocks in different colors; we made baskets out of cane kept soaking in a water butt outside the door. We tried out all the art forms that children usually try, and nobody interfered with our experiments or told us what to do, though advice and help were always available. It was clear to us that we were only beginners, but we knew it in a way that made us want to go on to learn more.

A child who spent any number of years at Beacon Hill would come away knowing a lot almost in spite of himself. Knowledge was all around us, and it was taken for granted that we would want to acquire it. A. S. Neill, founder of Summerhill School, wrote to my father, after reading his book on education: "I observe that you say little or nothing about handwork in education. My hobby has always been handwork, and where your child asks you about the stars, my pupils ask me about steels and screw threads. Possibly also I attach more importance to emotion in education than you do." He sums up nicely the differences between them: my father was hopeless at handwork and believed that the only appropriate emotion for learning was intellectual joy, whereas Neill, as far as I can see, tended to think of learning as dull textbook stuff, less exciting than living. For us it was never dull textbook stuff; it *was* living. We hardly ever used textbooks at Beacon Hill, except for math.

Besides being difficult, the material was often controversial. My father did not intend his education to be propaganda; he always wanted us to consider both sides and then make up our minds. "Considering both sides" meant hearing the opinions on both sides as well as studying the facts. Consequently, we were not subjected to those appallingly insipid "objective" presentations from which every possible element of controversy has been removed lest some parent might raise an objection. The bias of the teacher was always allowed to show, provided he or she took the trouble to present the other side also. In practice, at Beacon Hill, "making up our own minds" usually meant agreeing with my father, because he knew so much more and could argue so much better; also because we heard "the other side" only from people who disagreed with it. There was never a cogent presentation of the Christian faith, for instance, from someone who really believed in it.

From time to time the school experimented with keeping animals, but nothing really throve except the cats, who were fruitful and multiplied and went wild in the woods. At one time we had a donkey called Lucy, a shaggy grey beast we hoped to be able to ride. Donkeys are usually quite small and gentle, though they are stubborn, but this one was different. She tossed her head when you reached out to her, giving your hand a hard thump with her bony nose. And she got loose quite frequently and galloped about the lawns kicking up her heels and snorting. Then we would fetch my father down from his tower study, because none of us dared to approach her, and he would walk up calmly, as if he had been a donkey keeper all his life, take her by the halter and lead her quietly away.

One of the most important aspects of the school, for my parents, was its sexual freedom. I do not mean that we engaged in orgies—we were a little young for that—but that we were free to say anything we liked about sex, to ask any question and to compare ourselves with members of the opposite sex without concealment. We spent a lot of time discussing the differences between us and the relative advantages of being a boy or a girl. The boys were terribly proud of their urinating accuracy, which we girls greatly envied, but we always retaliated by saying, "Anyway, *you* can't make babies!" and that squelched them, because they wanted to.

Nobody frowned on such conversations or told us they were dirty. We talked about what was on our minds, and no topic was ever forbidden. New children from conventional schools, unused to such freedom, often went on a tremendous swearing spree when they arrived, using every dirty word they knew on every possible occasion. The rest of us listened with resigned amusement, knowing they would get over it as soon as they found it made no impression.

Of course boys and girls were treated equally at Beacon Hill. There was strong adult insistence on girls being as good as boys, and we were expected to be just as strong and brave and enduring as the boys, while they in turn were expected to learn to darn their own socks and to do simple sewing. Any differences between girls and boys were entirely of our own choosing, for the school policy treated us as though there were none. In practice, our close friends were usually of the same sex, though none of us objected to playing with members of the opposite one. Even a pseudo boy like me had girls for friends. I could play with boys, talk to them, work with them, love them or hate them; but I did not usually confide in them, whisper with them, share plans and secrets with them. Nor did the other girls. This was the way it happened, without any adult interference either way, and it was perfectly natural, because there was a biological difference of interest between us.

This was perhaps my mother's most valuable gift to the girls in her school. Having herself fought the battle of women's liberation, she freed us from the necessity of fighting it all over again. I do not mean that the battle is won in the world, but that we did not have to fight it in our own souls; we were not held back from worldly ambitions by false feelings of inferiority and subservience.

Many people read my parents' books and visited Beacon Hill and came away filled with enthusiasm. "This is the way it should be," they thought. "This is the right atmosphere of freedom and learning. This is success." As propaganda, it was very successful. As an example of what a school can be, also, but, judged in terms of my parents' hopes for the experience, did it fulfill their expectations?

Once, when I was young, my mother felt it necessary to sit down with me and say: "You know, Kate, you shouldn't try to correct people so often. They don't much like it when you tell them they are wrong."

To which I replied: "But I only tell them they're wrong when they *are* wrong."

I assumed they would be reasonable enough to see their error and to amend it, even to thank me for pointing it out. I assumed it because I had been taught to believe that people were reasonable and would respond to reason-

able argument. The whole school, and its promise for the
future, rested on this belief, as false and fantastic as any
religious superstition. Those of us who were pupils there
did not learn to rule our lives by reason (though we did
try), and we did not find, when we grew up, that the outside world responded with enthusiasm to our rational
arguments for reform. Many people (including ourselves)
preferred to cling to their errors.

I wrote earlier that we talked at school about what
was on our minds and that no topic was ever forbidden.
True and not true. We could talk about anything to anybody at any time, but only if we could put our feelings into
words. Thought and its expression were free, bad language
and rebelliousness were calmly tolerated, and we were allowed to say anything that we *could* say. But the fears we
were ashamed to acknowledge and the anxieties we could
not put into words had no outlet. For night terrors and
loneliness, for homesickness and fear of bigger children,
there was little that could be done. Even the youngest of
us had to manage our emotional lives pretty much alone,
without any close and sympathetic comforter. I learned to
get along inside a shell, fending off physical and emotional
assaults from others and trusting nobody. So did John, and
so, I think, did the other children.

Emotionally, the school was a bad experience for all
the Russell family. John and I felt turned adrift in a hostile
world, unable to go to our parents for help, and that feeling
remained with us always. John had been a very open little
boy, ready to talk anybody's ear off, but he changed; lack-
ing a friendly audience, he became wary and self-contained.
He and I learned to live in the middle, between parents
and children, slightly detached, keeping our own counsel,
cautious and unwilling to commit ourselves.

Our parents also suffered, feeling themselves cut off
from the children they loved so much. "The complete
happiness which had existed in our relations to John and

Kate . . . was destroyed, and was replaced by awkwardness
and embarrassment." The great outpouring of parental love,
which had made the Cornish years so happy, was stopped,
dammed up by worries and overwork and the obligation to
be just. My summer Santa Claus did not survive the school
years. Neither did the love of my parents for each other.

They came from Cornwall, full of joy and hope, to
start a school in which their children would blossom into
the finest flower of mankind. At the end of seven years,
they had lost each other, their children's confidence, their
money and much of their hope. Those years shattered the
crystal of our happiness and left us like jagged splinters,
unable to touch one another without wounding. All of us
longed for a give and take of love not possible in that public environment. Old pictures of my father with me on his
knee, holding my hand or putting an arm around me, strike
me as fakes. That is not the way I remember the school
years; they were all duty and loneliness and being just one
of the children, while all the time my father and mother
kept working, night and day, to preserve the school and
their separation from us.

My father in his *Autobiography* suggests that the
school gave nothing worth having in return for the grief it
caused. But he was always an absolutist; things that involved his emotions were either good or bad, and a school
that ate up his money and destroyed his family happiness
could not be good. He seemed to forget afterward the
good things that had happened at the school, as well as the
other causes of his troubles. My mother, on the other hand,
blamed circumstances and people, rather than the school,
for our family shipwreck, and she kept her commitment to
education long after my father had given up and moved on
to other things. She never believed that the school failed,
only that people failed to support it properly. In the same
way, she did not believe that her marriage failed, only that
others destroyed it.

For me personally, Beacon Hill School was an emotional disaster, because it smashed my bright world of childhood happiness and left me to spend the rest of my life searching for a replacement. But it gave much in return. Intellectually it was outstanding, and I learned more, with greater pleasure, in those years than I have learned anywhere since. Most of us there caught from my father something of the excitement of the things of the mind, which we could not have learned in any other school. It would be stupid of me to call it a failure simply because I was unhappy there. Nor was it all fear and misery; I remember a great deal of happiness from the years at Beacon Hill, both the ordinary pleasures of childhood and the intense satisfaction of mastering new skills. Skill of any kind was generously admired and praised, and so there was a double joy in acquiring proficiency: both one's own pride and the admiration of others. Since learning was not competitive, and we were never measured against each other by exams and grades, it was possible for us to be openly impressed by the achievements of others, which in no way diminished our own.

I remember, too, much pleasure in the association with other children: the excitement of wild twilight tag games, the fun of bouncing on the beds after lights out, the joy of making up a secret play with my friends and adding it to the end-of-term performances. Also the freedom of speech and the easy relations between boys and girls, children and adults, which I value more now than I did at the time, for then I knew nothing else.

Though loneliness and anxiety were my close companions through all those seven years, they do not seem to me too high a price to have paid for the intellectual excitement, the beauty and the exhilaration of learning we enjoyed.

Separation

Beacon Hill School began as a co-operative enterprise of two idealistic parents who seemed to have everything in their favor: enough money for a good beginning, an idyllic environment, a capable staff and my father's reputation. Working together, they could combine their differing talents to produce a stimulating atmosphere of experimental learning.

But unfortunately my parents were not together. When the school first opened, my father was away on a lecture tour in America, and my mother had to make all the precedent-forming initial decisions alone. The second term, she went off to America on a lecture tour to earn money, while he was left to run the school without her. Thus the enterprise was launched without adequate collaboration, and it continued in the same way. My father was off to America in pursuit of money again in 1929 and 1931, and when he was not in America he was busy writing books to raise the necessary funds. Even when they were both at school at the same time, its administration left them little opportunity for joint reflection on the way things were going.

I have little sense of time and rarely remember dates, but two stand out like tall trees from the tangled undergrowth of my childhood recollections: 1927, when the school started and the dissolution of our family began, and 1934, when John and I left our mother's Beacon Hill for Dartington Hall School, in Devonshire, and the process begun in 1927 was completed. The beginning of Beacon Hill School was for me the end of our family life, and the final separation of our parents from each other was hardly more devastating than this first separation of them from us, their children. In fact, I cannot even remember in what year they parted.

Was the school as responsible for their separation from one another as it was for ours from them? I do not think so, though their busyness with its affairs may have helped to conceal from them what was happening. I think the reasons were entirely personal. Here I must disappoint those readers who hope that I will now go into scandalous details about the marital troubles of my parents; even if I wanted to, I could not tell such things, because I do not know them. We lived, after all, in a school, among the other children. I cannot even remember where my parents slept, and of course I never knew with whom. In vacations, there were always other people about, friends and relatives and helpers, so that our parents' life with each other was quite separate from their life with their children. It was easy for them to enter into our world on terms of great affection and then withdraw again to conduct their private lives, generously sparing us any awareness of their problems. Consequently, my reconstruction is a retrospective interpretation of a child's view from below; large, dark gestures of rage and grief loom above me, but the tragedy takes place off stage, and I do not understand it or know the details of its unfolding.

Once my father had freed himself of his original puritanism, he was never again a one-woman man; though each new love might seem to be the ideal, he did not want to be irrevocably committed. "Love can flourish only as long as it is free and spontaneous," he said; "it tends to be killed by the thought that it is a duty." Like the sunshine, he could be loved while his warmth was upon you, but he could not be grasped and held. Those who tried found themselves with a shadow in their hands; the sunshine had escaped and was shining on someone else.

Being more of a philosopher than a psychologist, he supposed that his feelings were common to all mankind, and he elaborated them into the theory of marriage he expounded in *Marriage and Morals*. Though the book was considered an invitation to debauchery, it was in fact no more permissive than his educational theory. Here again, his innovation was in changing the rules, rather than abolishing them. In conventional marriage, man and wife promise lifelong devotion to one another and hope to keep that promise by resisting the temptation to pursue other partners; ideally, they do not even feel such a temptation. This seemed to my father an unnatural and unnecessary restriction, since most people are "generally polygamous in their instincts." "To say that it is your duty to love so-and-so is the surest way to cause you to hate him or her," he wrote. It was far better, in his opinion, to devote one's energy to subduing jealousy than to limiting the generosity of love. While a stable marriage was important for the children, the way to achieve it was by allowing freedom to one's partner, rather than by controlling one's own wandering inclinations. The new morality would be joyful and positive, but no less demanding than the old.

My parents' marriage was founded on these principles. They were equal partners, with equal freedom, joined together for the happy purpose of creating and raising children. "A marriage which begins with passionate love and leads to children who are desired and loved ought to produce so deep a tie between a man and a woman that they will feel something infinitely precious in their companionship, even after sexual passion has decayed, and even if either or both feels sexual passion for someone else." They were agreed on this. "A compact to have children," my mother said, "may involve very nearly a lifelong partnership, though not by any means strict marital fidelity."

They believed it would be easy to live without jealousy, but it turned out that the new morality was no easier and no more natural than the ideal of rigorous lifelong monogamy it was intended to replace. Calling jealousy deplorable had not freed them from it, any more than labeling his childish fears foolish had delivered John from their terrors. Nevertheless, it took my father a long time to acknowledge that he was expecting too much of human nature. "Anybody else could have told me this in advance," he wrote later, "but I was blinded by theory."

The theory was an attractive one, and it was not surprising that they were reluctant to give it up. A marriage based on trust and generosity, held together by the mutual affection of the parents for their children instead of by the rigidity of the law, would be a beautiful thing. It was hard to admit that the ideal had been destroyed by the old-fashioned evils of jealousy and infidelity.

My father had acknowledged, in *Marriage and Morals*, that if parents were quite unable to control their quarrels and conceal them from the children, it might be better for them to part. He thought the dissolution of a marriage "not nearly so bad as the spectacle of raised voices, furious accusations, perhaps even violence, to which many children are exposed in bad homes." Here again, he built a general theory out of personal inclination. As a boy, he had much preferred the hush of Grandmother Russell's house to the quarrels of Grandmother Stanley's, a preference which remained long after he had come to value intellectually the vigorous arguments of the Stanley household. He assumed that children would find family quarrels as devastating as he himself had and that, if it had become impossible to control or conceal such quarrels, his children must be living in a "bad home," from which it would be best to deliver them.

There were between my parents two fundamental disagreements, whose reconciliation would have required a degree of self-control and renunciation beyond even my father's exalted aspirations. First, my mother had two younger children who were not in fact my father's, though they might be considered his in law. Other people's children had never been part of the bargain for either of them. In recommending sexual freedom in marriage, my father was "of course assuming that the adulterous intercourse will not be such as to lead to children." In his particular case, though he might at that time have affected to despise such considerations, there was also the unpleasant possibility of having a non-Russell inherit the title and the family name.

My mother had agreed that a marriage that was a compact to have children would "quite clearly mean an honourable limitation on the woman's side, sufficient to insure the certainty of descent." I do not know how she came to change her mind about this agreement. Perhaps she never felt as strongly about it as my father did, for she tended to feel that a woman's children were her own affair and she did not have much sympathy for his aristocratic Russell pride. I never inquired because, having been brought up with my parents' emancipated views, I did not consider the arrival of my brother and sister shocking, or even odd enough to require explanation. Like the children quoted in my mother's book *In Defence of Children*, I would have remarked: "Why can't the threesome or foursome all live together in the same house? And of course they ought to have children, too, because the more children the better!" I knew nothing of the complicated agonies of adult emotions, for our parents never attempted to burden us with explanations of them. Consequently, I knew nothing at the time about the circumstances of my brother's or my sister's birth, and when I grew old enough to wonder I had become too sensitive to pry.

Perhaps my father might have accepted the children, out of kindness, out of human decency, out of unwillingness to destroy his family, had it not been for his second point- of disagreement, which was nonnegotiable. He had found someone else with whom he wanted to spend the rest of his life, not in an enlightened three- or four-way partnership, but in a comfortable old-fashioned, male-dominated marriage. His new love was Peter, who had charmed me completely when she first came to be our summer governess in Cornwall, the year my sister was born. She was one of the most beautiful women I have ever seen, when she was young; full of fun and zest for life. It was no wonder that my father fell in love with her. I loved her too, for her elegance, her femininity and her kindness to me, and I was delighted to see my father settle down with her.

Though my mother had to accept his decision to dissolve the partnership, she was never happy with it. Marriage had been a sacrifice for her, made in response to the importunity of my father's passion and the strength of her love for him. As she had feared, her personal aspirations had given way to the needs of husband and children, and she had found herself "just a wife," an appendage to a famous man, cut off beyond return from the ambitions of her youth. When their marriage of love and high ideals came to an end and she was left with nothing, she felt hurt and abandoned. Sometimes I feel her real life stopped at that point, with everything since a backward-looking "if only," an attempt to relive and change and understand those years with my father.

I have tried to describe the long dissolution of our home dispassionately, as my father would have wished. It was, however, a far from unemotional process, and all involved, including the children, emerged hurt, angry, bitter and desperately defensive. My father and mother lost much more than each other when they parted, and often it seemed easier to blame the other person than to admit that the whole optimistic scheme may have been wrong.

Perhaps the marriage was hopeless from the start, despite their love and good intentions. Tongue in cheek, my father later claimed his four marriages as proof that he approved of the institution of marriage. Maybe so, but I do not think it was a relationship that suited him, except in theory. All his life he sought perfection: perfect mathematical truth, perfect philosophical clarity, certainty of God's existence, a perfect formula for society, a perfect woman to live with in a perfect human relationship. And although he never found them anywhere, he never stopped looking. In his personal life, each new love roused new hope of an existence of harmonious bliss—and each time the woman proved to have defects which rendered it impossible. Rather than quarrel and compromise and "settle down," as people do who stay together, he would leave to search again for the ideal.

But what about the abandoned women? Somebody once asked him if it wasn't unkind of him to love and leave so many women.

"Why?" he asked. "Surely they can find other men too."

And he meant it. He could not imagine being the object of a woman's lifelong devotion. Though he loved many women and was loved by many, I do not think he ever felt lovable; he did not expect to keep a woman's love and he did not feel, in his heart, that she would lose much if he left her. This could make him insensitive and even unkind in dealing with someone he had ceased to care for. By the time he and my mother parted, he was so irritated by her that he had quite forgotten his former love. That chapter of his life was closed, and he was ruthlessly ready to start another, probably supposing that she felt the same.

My mother was, however, a very different person, and she did not feel the same. She is loyal and consistent and slow to change her mind, and when she gives her love she gives it forever, anything the beloved may do being somehow explained or excused or blamed on somebody else. She is as tenacious in love and hate as my father was fickle. They must have been like a sprinter and a cross-country runner harnessed together, and each in his way insensitive to the nature of the other; he to the lastingness of her attachment, she to the depth of his exasperation. Because she loved him, she wanted to believe him perfect. Because she enjoyed her freedom, she did not want to see that his nobility was inadequate to the demands she made on it, that, like any ordinary man, he was hurt and angered and wounded in his family pride by the arrival of cuckoos in the nest. Sometimes, listening to their complaints against each other, I used to wonder if they had ever understood one another, even at the height of their love.

While the last years my parents spent together were certainly years of turmoil for them, some of which we must have sensed, as long as they remained in one house they managed to preserve a united front before us. Most of the time they were able to act according to their belief that we should live lives of health and happiness and learning, untroubled by their adult preoccupations. Only after the separation did the awful business of self-justification and taking sides begin. It was not until those later years of our childhood that the currents of passion between our parents began to flow through us instead of meeting in sparks above our heads.

There was a summer, for instance, in our time of troubles that we spent at Hendaye, in the south of France, living in a kind of *ménage à quatre*. Peter was there as a combination governess to us and mistress to my father; my mother was there with her second daughter, then just a year old; the baby's father was there also, not living in the house but spending much time in it. It must have been a scene of considerable tension, yet my only memory of disagreement is of my father's distress at the way his rival wasted marmalade, which was essential to my father's breakfast and unobtainable locally. All my recollections are of summer pleasures and the strangeness of being abroad. My father took us on long walks in the mountains, brief excursions into Spain, small boat trips on the Bidassoa River, so cool and clear for swimming. On one of our mountain walks we accidentally crossed the border into Spain and arrived at a frontier post, where we were treated with great suspicion by the Spanish authorities, who thought we might be political smugglers and kept us waiting in the hot afternoon sun until they had convinced themselves we were the harmless English tourists we claimed to be. We sat on a bench in the dust beside the road, anxious and exasperated and trying to pretend it was funny, wondering if they would go so far as to put us in jail. That was the only adult anxiety I was aware of all summer.

On all these expeditions, John and I went with my father and Peter, which seemed to me perfectly natural, since Peter was still officially taking care of us and my mother was tied by the baby. Nor was I particularly surprised, when I went looking for Peter at night for comfort during the violent southern thunderstorms, to find her with my father. The way the grownups sorted themselves out was their own business. Mine was to find reassurance, and I sought it more readily from Peter than from my mother because I had given her my whole heart when she first came to take care of us in Cornwall the summer before.

Peter was young and energetic and absolutely imperturbable; during those first summers all our ingenuity could not devise ways of provoking her to anger. She charmed me particularly because she seemed to prefer me to John, a new experience. She listened to my stories, co-operated in my games and introduced me to the feminine mysteries of perfume and powder, nail files and cold cream. My mother used such things too and could have taught me had I asked, but Peter *invited* me to learn and made me feel I was being initiated into the art of being a woman. Though I wore boy's clothes in those days and had my hair cut short, so that most people took me for a boy, I *felt* like a girl, wanted to be a girl and loved learning from Peter about feminine adornment, even though I was unwilling to try it on myself. I had always imagined that my father liked John better than me, and I thought it might be because he was a boy, so that if at least I *looked* like a boy I might have some chance in the competition for his affection. It didn't work. I wanted to be loved for myself, as a girl, not as a substitute for John; besides, even if I had been able to replace him in my father's heart, I would not have wanted to do so.

My mother did things with us too that summer, different things. I recall her taking me to a swimming competition, where I received a very small medal on a thin blue ribbon, which was one of my chief treasures for a long time. We went down to the beach together, and I stood in the chilly brown estuary water with the little French children, anxiously watching the starter. "*Allez!*" he said, and all the others took off. I knew what it meant, but I wasn't *absolutely certain*, so I went on standing. "*Allez! Allez!*" he said, gesturing impatiently, and I lunged into the brackish water after the others. Luckily it was a distance test, not a race.

It was my mother also who made sure we were woken up at night and taken into Hendaye to see "the fiery bull." As part of the Basque summer festival, a model of a bull loaded with fireworks charged down the main street, glowing and flashing and banging, while its fiery eyes whirled round in its head and threw sparks in all directions. During the day, the Basque men in their brilliant costumes danced on platforms up above the spectators. To my fascinated eyes, they seemed to wind their legs around each other like ropes and then untwist them as they leaped in the air. I thought they must have some special kind of legs. They could drink without swallowing too, tilting their heads back and pouring the wine straight down their throats from wineskins. When I tried it, I choked and spluttered and soaked myself with water. These are the things I remember from that summer, not the awkward domestic problems of the adults.

After the separation things were different. Though there were still times of happiness, they were as precarious as a soap bubble, and a careless word could smash them. We had one more lovely summer in Cornwall, when my father was there with Peter, and we went to new places and did things we had not done before. Early one morning we drove to Penzance and took the white *Scillonian* to the Scilly Isles, where we stayed in a hotel on the island of St. Mary and rented a small boat to explore the varied beauties of the many other islands. I was seasick on the *Scillonian*, as I had been on the Channel steamer, while John was not; another distressing proof of his inherent superiority. From one of the islands we visited, we threw a bottle into the sea with the message "Help! Marooned on a rock off Samson Island, longitude ——— latitude ———." Many weeks later, we got a letter from a man on Lundy Island, far away in the Bristol Channel, politely hoping we had been rescued.

When we came back from the Scillys, we visited the Hole at Tolpedn and peered over its gravelly edge into the depths. The Hole (which always has a capital H in my mind) is a cave which has fallen in at the top, so that you can look down from above on the boulders and the churning waves below. Peter was wearing a wide straw hat, which blew off into the Hole—and in a moment, to our amazement, blew back out again. She at once claimed magical powers, insisted she was a witch and began throwing grass, leaves, handkerchiefs into the hole, with our eager assistance. At last, carried away by her own enthusiasm, she threw in a silver cigarette case to test her powers, but it dropped out of sight. Being still a young and relatively inexperienced witch, she could manage hats, but not cigarette cases.

That must have been the first summer my father and Peter were alone together; no wonder it was a time of jokes and folly and lightheartedness. But my father had no fixed occupation, and he and Peter had no home. He wondered where to go, what to do for money, how to start a new life at sixty. They spent a long, pleasant interlude at Deudraeth Castle, in North Wales, then an auxiliary to Clough Williams-Ellis's fantastic Portmeirion Hotel complex, and run with the same amiable efficiency as the main hotel.* The "castle" was fantastic too, in its own way: a

---

* In order to write letters to my father there, John and I had to learn to spell Deudraeth Castle, Penrhyndeudraeth, Merioneth, which we found quite a challenge. Once I had to call him on the telephone and had a dreadful time spelling Penrhyndeudraeth for the operator. The next day I had to call again and got the same operator. "Oh no!" she said. "Not that place again!"

nineteenth-century fake with turrets and battlements and castellated garden walls, all totally useless but wonderfully entertaining.

The castle had a rarely used library, where my father could work undisturbed, helped by Peter, who had no domestic duties to distract her from intellectual labor. He wrote *Freedom and Organization* there, and I can remember hearing him discuss with Peter the books they had been reading and the ideas he had. He would write, she would read what he had written and make comments, and occasionally he would change something she had not found clear. He changed things rarely and reluctantly and only for the sake of precision, for he thought out the whole structure of a book in his head before he began to write and did not like to tamper with individual portions of the total plan.

John and I were still attending Beacon Hill then, and we went to my father for vacations. Though it was very grand living in a hotel, with maids to make our beds and waiters to bring us our food, it made me nervous to have to behave so correctly all the time. Fortunately, since it was holiday time for us, my father would often put aside his work and accompany us on all-day expeditions into the mountains. Far up among the hills, in valleys beyond the reach of any modern road, we would come upon an old mine mouth or a grass-grown quarry, a row of tumble-down cottages, some rusty machinery, sometimes an owner's decent home, prim and gloomy and damp behind dark trees and garden walls. Down the headlong steep sides of the mountains ran the remains of tiny railways that once had carried out the slate so much in demand for building the drab industrial cities of England and Wales.

Walking in those mountains with my father meant much more than hiking up a trail to a peak, looking around and hiking down again. Before we set out, he would consider the weather, which is capriciously changeable among the mountains, and decide whether it would be a good day for an all-day expedition. I never learned his method, but it seemed to me foolproof; he didn't make mistakes about the weather.

He didn't get lost either. He owned and studied the ordnance survey maps for all of England, but I don't think he really needed them. He knew his direction by the sun, the wind, the landmarks. No matter how the mountains changed shape as we walked and viewed them from different angles, he always knew which they were. When we reached the top of a mountain, we identified every peak and lake we saw, and tried to name all the rivers and fix in our minds the relative positions of the different landmarks. This makes it sound a bit like a geography lesson, which it was not. It was more a matter of recognizing old friends seen from new angles and in different lights.

While my father taught us about weather and geography, Peter, who knew almost all the trees and flowers, taught us about the flora. Earlier, she had taught me the names of all the wildflowers in the Cornish hedges; now she made me acquainted with those of Wales, and if we met a strange one we would take it home to look it up in a book. Between the two of them, they surrounded us with familiar friends on all our walks. We saw the grand panorama, like any tourist, but we also saw and knew the details.

When the rain stops and the fog clears away, that corner of North Wales is one of the loveliest places in the world, and my father grew so fond of it that he chose to settle there at the end of his long life, in a house on the Portmeirion peninsula with a broad view across the estuary to the mountains and a house where Shelley once lived.

Somebody asked me recently why he chose to live in

such a remote place when he had so much important work to do in London. The question rather surprised me, for he usually lived in remote places, with a *pied-à-terre* in London for business purposes. He loved the country, he loved high hills and wide prospects, the changing of the seasons and the sweep of the weather, and he could not have lived for long in a city or a suburb. I suppose he need not have gone as far as North Wales, which is indeed inaccessible, but he loved it, had friends there and was not compelled by his work to be close to the center of things. Part of his good fortune and his greatness was that he usually managed to live surrounded by space and beauty, which gave him a peace and perspective he sorely needed. Without this rural solitude, he might have been overwhelmed by the griefs and perplexities of mankind, from which he was never able to detach himself with philosophic calm. Particularly in the last years of his struggle for peace, when he felt time running out for himself and for humanity, the view from Plas Penrhyn to the mountains brought calm to his troubled soul.

Living at Deudraeth Castle was delightful but expensive, and he and Peter could not stay there forever. The wisest course seemed to be to return to Telegraph House and live there until they could sell it. It was not easy for my mother to move the school elsewhere and to see her house, as well as her husband, taken over by her supplanter. However, it was not easy for my father to support her and his children and his wife (and one of his brother's wives too) on his depression-shrunken earnings. He thought he had no choice, and so, with bitterness on both sides, my mother withdrew, and he and Peter moved into the dilapidated, dirty and uninviting remains of Telegraph House.

Any building that houses a number of children grows battered and grubby in time, especially a progressive school which prefers damaged walls to damaged souls. My mother didn't care too much about cleanliness and tidiness anyway, for she was interested in producing fearless and beautiful human beings, not in playing caretaker to a gracious home. When we arrived, Telegraph House was in no condition to be sold as a gentleman's country residence.

Peter went to work on the house with energy and skill, and by the time she had finished it was altogether delightful. Betty's classroom now returned to its original function as library and sitting room and, although it was off by itself at the end of a long corridor, it became the heart of the house. My father had a huge desk in the bay window, where he sat and wrote all morning, spectacles on nose and pipe in mouth. Sitting on the sofa in front of the fire, I could watch him, when I was not reading, and observe the calm concentration with which he wrote. I was always a little afraid of him when he was working; he looked so Olympian. He did not hunch and fidget as I do, stare out of the window, cross things out, throw away sheets of scribbled paper. He simply sat up straight and wrote with his orange fountain pen until the tea came in at eleven o'clock.

Then he would move to his armchair by the fire, pour tea for everybody and tell us something interesting he had been reading or thinking. He would knock out his pipe, clean it, refill it, light it and sit there in perfect enjoyment until he had consumed the ritual three cups of tea and it was time to go back to work. He sat with his teacup held between both hands to warm them, a charming, familiar gesture known to all his family and friends.

Once, he told us, an old friend had brought his fiancée to tea to meet him, and as they sat making polite conversation the friend had suddenly interrupted, exclaiming: "Look, Janet! He's doing it. He's doing it now!"

"It" was holding the teacup in his own particular way.

After lunch, in accordance with my fathei's usual habit, we would go for a long walk. I have walked with my father in Wales and in Cornwall, in southern France and southern California, in Oxfordshire and Pennsylvania, on Dartmoor and on the Sussex downs, and those are only a fraction of the places he walked himself in his lifetime, either alone or in company. Wherever he lived, in the afternoons he walked and talked if he possibly could, being truly a peripatetic philosopher. At Telegraph House, where we could walk for miles through our own woods, cutting back brambles to keep the footpaths open and watching the dog in his inept chase after rabbits, my father enjoyed his new role of estate owner. He took great pleasure in walking about the place with a billhook, reopening the long-overgrown paths of his brother's time.

There was tea again in the afternoon, then more work until time for sherry before dinner. John and I were invited to partake of sherry, just as we were of tea and coffee. To us, it was simply an adult drink we could learn to like if we wanted to appear grown-up, not something special, dangerous or forbidden.

Dinner, thanks to Peter, was always an elegant occasion. We had a beautiful table and chairs (which had come to my father from the philosopher Wittgenstein),* heavy Russell family silver and candlesticks, glassware and china bought by Peter to complement them, and food worthy of the setting. Sometimes Peter and I would change into long

* Wittgenstein was a family name in my childhood as the giver of beautiful things, long before I knew of him as a philosopher. I used to picture his name as "Vitkenstein," and the first time I saw it written down I thought it must be some horrible mistake. When I was older, I used to hear my father speak of the importance of Wittgenstein's philosophy and the great difficulty of understanding it. Not long ago, I met a young man on a bus who told me he was studying philosophy and especially liked Wittgenstein. I suggested that he might be hard to understand. "Oh no," replied the young man. "I got a very good grade in the course."

John Russell, First Earl of Bedford, 1486(?)-1555

Photopress

Carn Voel, the "ugly house" in Cornwall,
where Kate and her brother John were happiest

John Russell at sixteen,
increasingly detached

Kate Russell at fourteen,
during "the barren years"

Bertrand and Dora Russell at Beacon Hill School
in the early '30's

(*Above, left*) Bertrand Russell, the lovely Peter, and their son, Conrad, 1939

(*Above*) On the porch at Beacon Hill

(*Left*) Kate, Bertrand Russell, Peter, and John at Yosemite
in the summer of 1939

John Russell in the navy, about 1944

Kate Russell as a graduate student, about 1947

Bertrand and Edith Russell, his fourth wife, with John's daughters, 1956

Bertrand Russell,
at the age of eighty-nine,
at Plas Penrhyn, 1961

Dora Russell, 1972

John Russell, 1971

Katharine Tait in Connecticut, 1973

housecoats for dinner. For me, it was the pinnacle of gracious living, the ideal way of life.

In the evenings at Telegraph House we often read aloud the solid old novels of Dickens and Walter Scott. Because my father and Peter both read beautifully, John and I never wanted to take a turn at reading. But we had to, and gradually learned to do it well, taking a quick look ahead to see the shape of a sentence before plunging in. My father did not consider anything well written that could not be read aloud, and he was convinced that one must appreciate the *sound* of good writing in order to write well oneself.

The orderly beauty of Telegraph House was due to Peter, who set the stage and managed the proceedings with great skill. Domestically my father was helpless; he did not know how to achieve the kind of environment he wanted and he was thankful to have it so pleasantly provided for him. After the chaotic, demanding, uncomfortable years of the school, it was restful for him to sink back into a quiet private life, cared for by a young, beautiful and devoted wife who appeared to put his interests before her own. Peter also helped my father with his work, and she took a lively part in all our conversations. I thought he had at last got someone to care for him properly, and when they finally had a child, in 1937, I imagined that their happiness must be complete.

However, I saw their life as an outsider. By my choice and theirs, I ignored the difficulties and saw only the pleasures. John and I were there as visitors, to be amused, cared for and convinced that this was a better home than our mother's. Not until I read my father's *Autobiography* did I realize how difficult the time at Telegraph House had been for him, the time when I thought he was so happy with Peter.

He was perennially short of money and did not know

which way to turn for more. His expenses had increased, the income from his books had decreased, nobody wanted to buy the house and nothing else offered itself as a possibility. All through the school years he had churned out popular books and articles to make enough money to keep the school going, repeating many times his views on education, marriage, politics and the possibilities of science. Now he was tired from the long years of strain, and also uncertain of what to say. Free marriage had proved more difficult than he had expected, its failure painful and expensive. Was he to go on recommending it to others? Parental love remained as strong as ever, but its proper expression in a divided family posed a problem. In any case, he felt that he had failed as a parent and could hardly keep on advising others. What could he say about education without sitting down and reviewing his theories at length? And now that he was no longer head of a school or a full-time parent, why should he trouble to do so?

Marriage and education were no longer acceptable topics, but what about politics? He had been active in politics for many years, had written innumerable articles and books in which he applied his sharp intelligence to the solution of social and political problems. The world of the thirties certainly offered problems enough: unemployment at home and imperial oppression in India, vicious civil war in Spain and totalitarian brutality in Italy and Germany. I remember my father explaining to us that, much as he loved Italy, he could not take us there, because Mussolini had said that anyone who offered Bertrand Russell hospitality would be imprisoned. I remember anguish over Franco and efforts to help the Spanish refugee children, struggles to get Jews out of Germany and political prisoners out of Germany and Russia, attempts to help their bereaved families with money and sympathy.

He did everything he could, but it was no more than

first aid. Though it helped individuals, it gave him little satisfaction, for he longed to reorganize society along rational lines, instead of merely assisting the casualties of the existing system. Formerly, he had been confident of his ability to do so, but in those years of personal uncertainty he grew to doubt the wisdom of his political solutions also. There seemed no simple way to combine individual freedom with economic justice and the international government he considered essential to the preservation of peace. Like relations between the children in the school, relations between nations and classes proved resistant to rational reorganization. Human folly and wickedness were powerful and entrenched, and it was difficult indeed, during the years of Hitler's power, to maintain a belief in the possibility of a benevolent and reasonable society. Worse still, there seemed no peaceful way of dealing with the monstrosities which had grown up in Germany and Italy. My father had been a pacifist since long before the First World War, and his pacifism, born in a moment of mystical experience, was as strong as a religious faith—and as irrational. It had sustained him through all the trials of the First World War, including prison, and he took its continued existence for granted, maintaining in his book *Which Way to Peace?* (written in 1936) that passive resistance would disarm aggression, and using Gandhi's achievement against the British in India as his example. It was the first book of his I ever read, and I found it utterly convincing. Surely, I thought, in view of these facts, no government would be mad enough to start another war. But my father was less convinced by his arguments than I, and he never allowed *Which Way to Peace?* to be reprinted, feeling that it was insincere. He had no objection to reprints of books maintaining views he had since abandoned, but this one maintained a view he had not really held even while he was writing it. As it became clear to all who followed the news that the Nazis were in no way disarmed by passive resistance, my father began to have second thoughts about his pacifism, and so another field of action was closed to him. He could neither support nor condemn attempts to build up Britain's military power in opposition to Hitler.

When John and I came home on vacation, we saw none of this, for we did not look beneath the surface. Even if we had wanted to, such prying would have been unwelcome; though joy was to be shared, distress he considered private.

To take his mind off insoluble personal or political problems, my father had a hierarchy of distractions, the most elementary of which was the steady routine of daily life. The next, a constant distraction through all the years I knew him, was what he called "silly books." Wherever we went, a first priority (in the days before paperbacks) was to find a lending library with a large supply of detective stories to occupy his leisure hours. He often read a book a day, and it hardly mattered if the books were bad, since they were meant to provide complete mental relaxation. They were not called "silly books" for nothing. Troubles too insistent to be banished by frivolous reading could sometimes be suppressed by mathematical or philosophical problems difficult enough to demand complete concentration, the next step up on the ladder of distractions.* When all these failed, he could sometimes forget incurable personal griefs by immersing himself in the struggle against public wickedness. This is not to imply that he undertook public activity as a means of escape from private unhappiness. Quite the contrary. His political actions arose always out of his passion for justice and his sympathy for suffering,

---

* "For about two months, purely to afford myself distraction, I worked on the problem of the twenty-seven straight lines on a cubic surface. But this would never do, as it was totally useless and I was living on capital." So he wrote *Which Way to Peace?* instead.

and he was generous enough to take comfort from giving happiness to others when he could not obtain it for himself.

In the thirties, however, even this comfort was limited to personal acts of kindness to people in trouble. He could find no way to help the world, no way even to help his family, so he tried another distraction: he wrote, with Peter, an account of his parents' brief lives, which he called *The Amberley Papers*. His parents had been admirable people, who did what was right in a simpler and more hopeful world, and it gave him pleasure to publish an appreciative memoir of their beliefs and actions, as they had recorded them in diaries and letters. However, as he says in his *Autobiography*, he regarded this work as an escape from reality and therefore "not really important."

"Really important" work meant improving the lot of mankind or making a permanent contribution to philosophy, and even the most exquisite private happiness would not long have contented him without one or both of these more impersonal satisfactions.

He began to think of going back to philosophy, feeling that his ideas had changed somewhat, that he had a new contribution to make to the philosophy of meaning. But he could not afford to do so without a paid position. He went so far as to inquire if there was any possibility of a return to Trinity College, Cambridge, which had dumped him for his pacifist activities during the First World War— a humbling of his pride to which only desperation could have driven him. As he expected, the answer was no. At that point, Oxford fortunately invited him to give a course of lectures on philosophy, in which he was able to develop his new ideas under the pleasantly simple title "Words and Facts."

Meantime, the rest of his family had other problems. In those years, each of us was locked in isolation with his own troubles, looking for sympathy and support from others and unable (or unwilling) to give any to them. John and I stayed on at Beacon Hill for a while after my father left, but we found it dreary and began to complain to him, telling him for the first time about the ferocious teasing of John, which had grown even worse. For the first time we had a parent able to listen because not involved with the school; indeed, my father was all the more willing to listen because our complaint involved criticism of my mother. Consequently, he insisted on removing us from the school and sending us away to Dartington, where he hoped we would be happier.

Dartington was a very good school. The headmaster believed in reasonableness, moderation and sound learning, and his belief set the tone for all of us. We had a high degree of self-government and individual freedom, which rarely degenerated into aimlessness and license, either in class or out. There were fixed rules, based on age, about bedtime and pocket money and a few other matters, but beyond that most things were managed by the enlightened common sense of the school council.

From then on, things got better, and we were indeed happier than at Beacon Hill. The teaching was good, the atmosphere pleasant, and Dartington had one great advantage over Beacon Hill: enough money. Having been started by L. K. and Dorothy Elmhirst as part of the Dartington Hall Estate, the school was as well provided for as all their other enterprises. The heart of the estate was the Hall itself, a magnificent medieval manor house resting calm and gray in the midst of unbelievable gardens. The Elmhirsts added money and imagination and a dominant idea: to create a cultural center in rural surroundings, a place devoted to excellence in all the arts and crafts, where people could live with and create beauty.

The cultural advantages of the school, however, were not the cause of my contentment; other aspects of school life meant much more to me. I could live detached there,

with nobody making emotional demands on me, retiring
to my own room with a book whenever I liked and following my own routine, which could include or exclude others
as I chose. Classes were interesting, living was comfortable,
the environment was lovely and it was a blessed relief to
be able to live for a while away from the unspoken demands of home and the frightening tensions of Beacon
Hill.

"Children whose actual home has been changed or
dissolved" by divorce, my mother wrote, "will . . . need
some refuge from home life, in school, and, if possible,
boarding school. There they can rest their nerves and see
the home situation in truer perspective." When she wrote
this, she was thinking of her own school as a refuge for
children of other divorces; although she did not see it quite
the same way when it came to her own, she was nevertheless right.

Dartington had little to do with my father's life, but
much to do with mine; it preserved my sanity, educated
my mind and trained my sense of beauty. It provided an
atmosphere of placid tolerance and a stable environment,
when both my homes were changing.

When the lists went up at school, at the end of the
term, telling who was to go by which train and whose luggage had to be ready first, all the children got excited and
restless and began to long for home. I, however, began to
think anxiously of the tensions awaiting John and me in
both our homes. For us, each school vacation was exactly
divided in half, even to the half day if it happened to have
an odd number of days, and we moved from one house to
another like pawns, pretending to have no feelings. We
played elaborate games of pretense with each other: the
comparison of homes was in everyone's mind, yet it was
rarely mentioned. Confrontations were to be avoided at all
costs.

Even now, I cannot write about those years with detachment. The old bitterness rises and flows out of my pen as I recall the anxiety and unhappiness John and I felt whenever we stayed in either home. Our parents were unhappy, disappointed and unsure of themselves. They wanted to do what was best for us and, not unnaturally, they were anxious that we should appreciate their good intentions. Unfortunately, they disagreed about what was best for us and could not refrain from fighting over our welfare. We, who had been the field of their joint endeavors at human reform, became the battleground for their now opposing theories of child welfare. Indeed, their civilized tolerance had been so totally consumed that they could communicate with each other only through lawyers, turning every trifle into a major disagreement.

A word from us of what the other parent thought could bring on an endless explanation from the one to whom we spoke. I can remember still the sick, trapped feeling I used to get when some careless word of mine brought on a speech of self-justification, which could be ended only by assent, whether genuine or feigned. I would sit politely, agreeing when it seemed unavoidable, all the time inwardly poised for flight and casting round for any excuse to escape the terrible demand for approval.

When I was twelve years old or thereabouts, I became nearsighted; I could no longer see the blackboard unless I sat in the front row of the classroom. My friends and I knew this, but I did not want the authorities to find out, because I knew they would tell my parents, and I did not want to seem less than perfect in my father's eyes. I also dreaded the amount of adult attention I would inevitably incur. Eventually one of the teachers found out, and the school arranged to take me to an eye man in a nearby town, who subjected me to the curious and rather frightening rigamarole that oculists put one through. At the end of it all, he said: "You have one-sixth of normal sight and you will have to wear glasses all the time for the rest of your life."

I rode back to school in despair, trying desperately not to cry in front of the teacher and on a public bus. I wrote anguished letters to both my homes, looking for comfort. I should have known better. The consequence was that each parent took me to another doctor and I got three examinations instead of one, plus a lot of unpleasant fuss.

Such episodes were a bitter substitute for our previous happiness. And we also had to cope with our own personal disappointment. We had imagined our parents to be superior in every way to the conventional: *our* parents would never quarrel sordidly over conjugal rights or the way to bring up children; they were far too generous and intelligent. Yet there they were, not only doing these things, but even trying to involve us in their disagreements. It was sickening. The only solution was inward withdrawal, my father's old tactic. It was at that time that I came to regard progress, like Santa Claus and the Easter bunny, as a myth of childhood, and I have never since believed in any utopian project of any kind.

Although my parents did not draw quite such extreme conclusions, they felt the failure of their enterprise keenly and watched our progress anxiously to see if they had done us any harm. I used to feel an obligation to keep on functioning admirably in order to reassure them. I do not know whether John felt the same, for he never told me. We had gradually become as reticent with one another as with our parents.

Sometimes, when my mother had first turn, it would still be term time in her school when we got home from Dartington, and the place would be full of unknown children and staff living their unknown lives. There seemed no place for us in the school routine. Term ended after a few days and these strangers dispersed to their own homes, leaving us alone and without much to do in our corner of whatever country mansion the school was in. I hated the uncertainty of it all, the lost, unbelonging drifting round a big house I never knew well. And I showed it. I sulked incessantly, glooming about with a huge chip on my shoulder, barely speaking. I don't know how my mother stood it.

My mother ran the school alone for about ten years, during which she had sole responsibility both for its operation and for the care of her two younger children. She received money from my father, but no other kind of support from anyone. Though she had many admirers, dependents, employees and hangers-on, there was nobody for her to turn to in times of desperation. I do not know how she managed to survive and keep the school afloat. She must have been frantic with worry and loneliness, but she never complained to us, and we offered her no sympathy.

Once at Carn Voel, during a vacation, I woke in the night in my third-floor bedroom and heard her sobbing downstairs. I got up and went down to see if there was anything I could do. When she heard my footsteps on the stairs, she pulled herself together with a great effort, wiped away the tears and looked toward the door as I came in.

"Is there anything wrong, dear?" she said.

"Oh no . . . I just couldn't sleep. . . ."

What else could I say? I trailed away back to bed, frustrated in my good intentions, unable to penetrate her defenses.

All through the Dartington years I disliked and despised my mother. I cringed when she came to visit us and tried to hide her from my friends. She used to buy old secondhand cars for ten pounds or so and drive them till they died, sitting at the wheel in her shabby and eccentric clothes, squinting through the smoke of a lipstick-stained cigarette whose ashes dropped into her lap as she drove, and laughing her hearty, raucous laugh as she made light of conventional manners and morals. She would sit through "God Save the King" in cinemas, sing the "*Inter-*

nationale" in public places, march in Communist demonstrations, while I shrank into myself and tried to pretend I didn't know her. With the harsh intolerance of childhood, I despised her and shut her out of my life, which was happily filled by my love and admiration for Peter and my father.

I am ashamed of my unfairness. When my mother had married my father, she had been young and beautiful like Peter, fond of clothes and dancing and the admiration of young men. She too had made him a beautiful home, in Cornwall, and had built her life around him, fully expecting to stay with him always. Now that she found herself abandoned for someone younger, left alone with her memories and her responsibilities, how could she be the calm and gracious beauty my adolescence demanded? It was much that she did not break down, never played the pathetic martyr, never burdened us with her troubles or looked to us for the affection she had lost.

Nor was that all. Like my father, she had an immense zest for living, a capacity for laughter and enjoyment, which no amount of worry could subdue. She shared with us as much of her joy as we would accept.

She took us to Paris once, a city full of happy memories for her from old student days, before she married my father. She rushed us about from pleasure to pleasure like a caretaker in paradise, inviting us to participate in her delighted appreciation of the absurd as well as the sublime. I remember her, with John, cheerfully jumping off a tower by parachute at the Exposition fair, a feat far beyond my courage. I do not think she was afraid at all.

That happy expedition to Paris became another bone of contention between my parents, because John and I were not supposed to be taken out of England without the agreement of both parents and the Court of Chancery.

In emotional moments, my mother used to say that she would like to take us all off to live among the sensible people of Russia, which had been her dream country since her romantic expedition there in 1920. I doubt if she would have put the dream to the test of reality, but my father, who had seen her go there once against all expectations, was never sure. He was terrified that she would take us off to Russia, where she would soon be in prison for opening her mouth, leaving his children derelict and inaccessible. So he had us made wards in chancery, which meant that we needed the permission of both parents and the court before we could leave the country. It was a tiresome restriction, which kept us tied to England, and I always thought it a piece of needless caution on my father's part. Though my mother liked to dream of a brave new life in Russia, she was wise enough not to attempt it with four young children in tow. However, it was useless to try to convince him of that. His bitterness made him obdurate in his suspicions.

When my father at last succeeded in selling Telegraph House, he went with Peter and Conrad (my younger brother, then a baby) to live near Oxford, where he was to lecture on philosophy. He bought an old house, in the village of Kidlington, which Peter's gifts soon turned into another beautiful home. It was a lovely house, with exquisite walled gardens, but to me it will always be a place of great unhappiness. The year we spent at Oxford was a time of bitter division for us all: faultfinding between our parents and cautious silence between John and me. During that year, my mother committed the awful offense of keeping us an extra half day in one vacation—and the angry response from my father and Peter made me wonder for the first time about their perfection.

Also, in that year, John began to detach himself from all of us, keeping his own counsel and living his own private life. Until then, I had felt that John and I were two against the world; family bitterness had overshadowed our early rivalry, and we had joined together to protect ourselves from adult demands. But behind our mutual-defense pact lay real differences between us, for John never got on easily with Peter and sympathized much more with our mother than I did. I tried to talk to him about it all sometimes, until his brief and noncommittal answers made me realize that he saw the situation differently and didn't want to discuss it. I wonder now if I ever really knew John, who had been there from the first day of my life as my hero and my rival, the embodiment of strength and success and all that was good in life. My childhood ambition, never quite discarded, had been to be his house-keeper when we grew up; he would be prime minister and I would take care of him, and we would always be to-gether. (I also intended to write successful books under a pseudonym and one day to be called out of John's shadow into the glare of public adulation.) I don't know what John's ambition was. For all his chattering, his private life was secret.

The house in Kidlington had a pair of two-room cot-tages attached to it, which were fixed up for John and me, since the house itself was not big enough for all of us. I had the cottage nearest the house and John the end one. There he stayed much of the time, in untidy isolation, pro-tecting himself from adult demands for loyalty and other assaults upon his emotions. When he wrote to me many years later, at a time of great personal distress, that he didn't want to belong to anyone's "rah-rah gang," my mind went back to that Kidlington cottage and John hiding there like an animal at bay. It was all much worse for him than for me.

One day, in one vacation spent at Oxford, my father called me to him with evident embarrassment, looked at me earnestly and said: "Kate, it seems to Peter and me that you don't wash your face in the morning. Really you should, you know. It's dirty not to."

I was humiliated. I flushed crimson, feeling as though

I had been reproved for some deadly sin, too ashamed to reply. To be sure, he achieved his desired result: I have washed my face every morning from that day to this; but the price was high. That trivial scene raised a barrier of embarrassment between us, which I have been unable to laugh at until now. It was typical of that year, during which trifles persistently grew into major emotional issues, though never into scenes.

In that house too my father explained to me one day that he found it best to have a set routine for things like shaving, dressing, emptying and filling his pockets, so that he never had to think about them. I thought that was foolish of him, because the routine became a sort of prison from which he could not escape. It seemed to me much better to be flexible and free. Perhaps that was the first time in my life I ever consciously thought I knew better than he did. I suppose I was growing up.

After a year at Oxford, my father accepted a position at the University of Chicago and went off again to America, the land that had always taken him away from us. This time it didn't seem so bad, for we were older, we had Dartington, and there were frequent letters—short, neat ones from my father and long, sprawling, funny ones from Peter. He showed us before he left how to look in the paper to find out when the *Queens* were sailing and when to mail our letters to be sure of catching them, so that communication was rapid and reliable. Nevertheless, it was a bad year for me personally, a year of change and doubt, in which I needed much moral support. And my father was gone again; he was never there when I needed him. Worse, he had taken Peter with him, in whom I had put all my trust when parents seemed to fail me. I would not have considered turning to my mother, who was one of my problems. I wrote long, morbid letters, which they answered very kindly, but the exchange took two weeks and was always incomplete, so that by the time John and I joined them in America I had lost the habit of confiding in them. Feelings were hurt, for I was sullen as well as uncommunicative, but I felt I could not help it.

The year my father spent at Chicago was 1938, the year of Munich. It was agony for him to be out of England, powerless to affect events, with two children left behind to face the danger of war. He felt his pacifism crumbling in his soul as he contemplated the possible devastation of his country and listened to the callous comments of un-involved Americans. Nevertheless, he went on educating and entertaining his students, writing me encouraging let-ters, playing with Conrad, going to dinner parties, never revealing the anguish he lived with.

After he left Chicago, he was to teach philosophy at UCLA. He had arranged with my mother that we should spend the whole of the Christmas and Easter vacations with her, then join him in California for the summer, returning to England in September to go back to Dartington. But that was September of 1939. It seemed folly to send us back to England when others were frantically trying to get their children out, so we stayed on with my father, and the period of my life that I think of as "the barren years" came to an end.

There were five barren years, from 1934 to 1939. John was almost thirteen when they began; I was almost eleven. They were the unhappiest years of my life, a time of set-tled misery so deep and pervasive that I was barely con-scious of it. The parents whose help I needed seemed al-ways to be wanting mine instead. Over and over they assured us that they wanted to do what was best for us, only the other parent was mistaken about what the best was. I believed them, but I didn't like being asked for my approval when I wanted to ask for theirs. I wished they could see us as ourselves, not as part of the battle with the other parent. Sometimes I felt we were never ourselves to them, but embodiments of a cause: first in their fight against convention, and then in their fight against each other.

Deep underground in my soul, I wanted to say: "Look at me. I'm a girl. I like to dress up and be pretty. I want to grow up to be a mother. Admire me, like me, enjoy me as I am. I don't really want to be a public hero, I'm not clever enough to be a great brain, I'd rather be a girl than a boy." But I said no such thing. I was hardly aware that I thought it. I said and did what I thought my father wanted, and I felt it would be selfish to ask for praise or even for recognition of my merits.

"Selfish" . . . one of the most powerful words of my childhood. I believed that to talk about "me" was a sign of selfishness. Since I couldn't think of anything else to talk about, I kept quiet. I believed that demanding a fair share of anything, pointing out any achievement of one's own, was selfish. One should always do one's outstanding best, and then say: "Oh, it was nothing. I only did my duty." I believed one should love and serve without hope of reward or return of affection, because no one deserved to be loved who was not totally unselfish. Only through self-abnegation could I attain the affection I craved, which would then be showered upon me as largesse. Though he would have repudiated this crude statement of them, these were my father's beliefs. They were not realistic. They made difficulties for him, they have made difficulties for me, they made difficulties between us. I wish he could have been satisfied with less.

The five barren years ended on the day in August 1939 when John and I set sail for America on the *Queen Mary* to spend the rest of the summer with our father. As I stood high on her deck, watching Southampton dock receding into the distance, I felt I was escaping from a nightmare. This time *I* was going to America and others were being left behind with their sorrows.

California

Somewhere among my belongings I have a box of old photographs that has traveled around the world with me from home to home. At the bottom, as completely concealed as possible, lies a picture taken from the deck of the *Queen Mary* as she moved away from Southampton dock. There on the dock stands my mother, smiling and crying and waving a handkerchief, plagued with worries, frantic with eczema. Next to her my half brother and half sister, looking sulky and bored and vaguely unhappy. Then her strange sister Mary, with whom we had been staying, and some of Mary's awkward boys, in baggy English schoolboy raincoats. I kept the picture hidden for years. It was one of my most shameful secrets, yet I never threw it away.

I stood at the rail waving dutifully, knowing how much such ceremonies meant to my mother, but my heart was dancing, my spirits lifting with the wind, as we moved out into the ocean. How glad I was to get away! How much more at home I felt in the grandeur of the *Queen Mary* than in my mother's grubby surroundings. At last I was waving good-bye to grief and on the way to rejoin the two people I loved most, sailing off into the great world to which my father belonged.

It was lucky for me I could not see myself as others did. All my grand imaginings would have crashed to the ground if I could have seen what Peter saw when we arrived: a fat, pasty girl, with straggly hair and glasses, dressed in whatever I could find that would cover my awkward shape, lumping along with downcast head and turned-in toes. I knew I was not beautiful, but until I saw myself with Peter's disappointed eyes I did not realize that I had grown ugly.

In New York we were met by my father's publisher, Warder Norton, and his wife, Polly, who showed us the principal sights of the city, fed us and put us on the train to San Francisco, where my father planned to meet us. He and Peter were waiting for us at the station when we arrived there. How reassuringly familiar they were in that strange place! What a relief not to be on our own any more. Novelty was much more enjoyable under my father's protection and with Peter there to share my thoughts.

They had bought a car, a secondhand two-door Chevrolet, which looked to me like a luxury limousine, and we set off for a holiday at Yosemite.

Yosemite was lovely, but it was HOT, a new experience and one I didn't much like. We stayed in a hotel in the park surrounded by pine trees, where we were roused early in the morning by the sun blazing in our windows, bringing with it the powerful aroma of hot resin and pine needles. I drooped around all day, damp and prickling, looking for sympathy from Peter in my discomfort. But things had changed.

"You know you always made fun of me for feeling the cold," she said. "Now you are minding the heat. Some people can stand heat and some can stand cold. Now you can perhaps understand my discomfort."

I sulked. But Yosemite was too magnificent to be sacrificed to hurt feelings. We drove to a mountain camp so high that our breath came short at first, and it was a day or two before we could join an all-day hiking party, to be guided up the most accessible peak by a charming and well-informed young ranger. Though my father was sixty-seven, we took it for granted that he would go with us, walking uphill all morning and down over rough rocks in the afternoon. If he ever got tired, he never showed it.

From Yosemite, we went to Santa Barbara, to stay in a cool creeper-covered cottage, set in a green garden surrounded by hedges, and very comfortable. When teatime came on our first day there and tea came with it, it seemed to me as though we were at home together again. But it was all different. The cups and spoons were odd shapes, the food was wrong and the tea was made and served by a large black cook called Mary, stern and forbidding and easily offended. We never knew what would provoke her, so we were always on edge for fear of annoying "the help."

At the beginning of our stay in America, we had various kinds of "help," but we never managed to hit it off with them. First they would grow sullen and then they would disappear, and we could never find out why. It was almost a relief when the war dried up the supply of domestic servants, even though none of us enjoyed housework or did it with any particular skill. Except Peter. Though she did not enjoy it either, she certainly knew how to make a house gleam and how to put a good meal on the table. I learned a lot from helping her, however reluctantly.

Santa Barbara smelled of oil all the time. It looked cool and green and lovely, but the heavy smell of oil hung in the air like poison. I felt as if an industrial landscape had been cunningly disguised as a residential area, for oil meant cities and factories, and I could not connect it with gardens and beaches, even though I knew intellectually that I was in oil country.

During our stay there, my father hurt his back and had

to lie flat and in pain for what seemed a very long time. Peter found a doctor, a young and charming neighbor, who soon became our friend, continuing to visit us after it was no longer professionally necessary. Even in my cocoon of adolescent self-absorption, I couldn't help noticing how Peter flirted with him, though I was too innocent to think anything of it and too wrapped up in myself to care much. Nevertheless, I felt uncomfortable when she used me as a foil to her charms; the Santa Barbara doctor was another small crack in her image.

Toward the end of August 1939 we moved down to Los Angeles, where my father was to start teaching at UCLA in September. A house was found, the move made, decisions arrived at in a sort of waking nightmare of political anxiety. Everything was done between news broadcasts. My father and Peter knew there would be war and they were sure their beloved England would be destroyed while they were away, living in an unwilling safety forced on them by responsibility for their children. They sat by the radio with drawn faces, listening desperately for news and getting only fragments interrupted by jolly commercials.

I was not interested in the news. I was sure there would not be war; grownups could not be so stupid. I did not see why the others worried so and lost sleep over it, for surely something would be arranged. I closed my ears and my mind to the chattering of the radio news and stubbornly refused to listen. But war came anyway. Sitting at the far end of the living room in numb dismay, I had to hear at last what the commentators were saying and recognize the reality of war.

This was not what I had been taught about mankind. Despite his doubts, my father had taught us to hope, to believe in progress and to work for it. He had not pretended it was automatic, but he had certainly made us believe it was possible. When war came, I felt bewildered and betrayed and as desperately unhappy as my father had in 1914, but I dealt with my despair in a different way. Because my father was already forty years old before the First War began, a mature man with a settled view of life, he was able to come through the nightmare with his ideals battered but intact, and he could teach them to his children without skepticism.

I was only fifteen in 1939, still learning what the world was like, and I learned from the war a lesson which would not have pleased my father if I had told him of it. My conclusion can best be summed up by the Russell family motto, *Che sara sara* ("What will be, will be")—a motto that suits me far better than it does my father. There are no good or evil sides, I thought, and no good or evil people, only varying degrees of stupidity and greed, mercy and generosity. No cause seemed so pure as to be worth my devotion; therefore it seemed best to live a quiet, private life, doing what personal good I could and perhaps, through having children, contributing to the number of good people in the world. I was ashamed of this pusillanimous ambition, yet I had seen enough, in my own short life, of the unfairness of extremes and the damage done by zeal to feel that a little quiet domestic healing was not necessarily the worst thing I could do.

My idealism was not helped by my father's apparent abandonment of his pacifist position and acceptance of the necessity of war. From six thousand miles away, he faced the possibility that England might be devastated by bombs and overrun by the Nazis. All his friends might be killed and every place he loved destroyed, and he could neither do anything about it nor even be there to share in the tragedy. As the "phony war" went on and he endured the insensitive jokes of uninvolved Americans, he suffered agony. "I found this possibility" of utter defeat "unbearable," he wrote, "and at last consciously and definitely decided that I must support what was necessary for victory in the Second World War, however difficult victory might be to achieve, and however painful its consequences."

He believed that reason had led him to support the Second War, while his emotions "followed with reluctance." I believe the division in his mind was less between reason and emotion than between conflicting emotions: love of country versus love of peace. My father's love for England was deep and passionate, perhaps his strongest emotion. One would have thought, to see his anguish at that time, that his dearest love was chained to a rock and awaiting the approach of the dragon. So she was; and he, the hero, was not free to go to her rescue, because he had a wife and children to provide for. I felt the reproach of my existence keenly. No, it was not reason that led him to support the war; nothing was decided on rational grounds in those last months of 1939, when we moved like sleepwalkers through a dream of death.

Yet decisions were made and life went on. We woke up and noticed the house we had taken, a Spanish-type villa with an enclosed garden and olive trees. Though not large as we judged size, the house was fantastically luxurious: dressing room and bath for every bedroom, deep soft rugs, and shelves and shelves of fancy linens and dishes. Luxury, but not the kind of comfort we were used to. To a certain extent, the owners' style of living forced itself upon us, as though we were wearing other people's clothes. I felt wretchedly ill at ease in my frilly pink-and-white girl's bedroom, surrounded by mirrors and daintiness. During that ugly-duckling phase of my life, I preferred to ignore my appearance and concentrate on the keenness of my mind.

Hoping to hasten my development into a swan, Peter took me to a doctor, who weighed me and measured me and asked a hundred questions, then put me on an eight-hundred-calories-a-day diet, which consisted almost exclu-

sively of lettuce and cottage cheese and tomato juice. I
hated it. Miserably hungry and sorry for myself, I sat at
meals with my teaspoonful of food, balefully watching the
others eat. Then I discovered the wonderful world of American candy bars spread out and waiting for me at every
drugstore counter, and found that for only a nickel I could
buy half a day's calories in chocolate and nuts. The doctor
wondered why I stopped losing, but I didn't tell him.

Peter really took me in hand during those first months
in America, cutting off my straggling hair, putting me on
that diet, buying me new clothes and seeing that they suited
me. I looked better when she was finished, but I still *felt*
awkward. She had a way of emphasizing the drawbacks she
was showing me how to conceal, leaving me more than
ever conscious of them. I don't think she did it deliberately; the stepmother was so much lovelier than Snow
White that she had no need to. But she did enjoy being
lovelier—naturally!—and left me well aware of my own
disadvantages.

Gradually, as we came to know more about America,
we realized that the people who owned our house must be
rich, though its small size and lack of books had at first
deceived us. John and I, who had led sheltered, Spartan
lives, found ourselves living in a pampered luxury we only
partially enjoyed. We had tended to assume at first that
everything we saw was simply "the American way of
doing things," and we looked at it with an open mind, making no moral judgments. However, as we came to understand more about the price paid by others for the comfort
in which we lived, we liked it less and less. Peter read
books about the migrant workers, about business exploita-
tion and crooked land deals, and she told us with indignation what she had learned. But we went on living in
comfort just the same, not feeling ourselves responsible
for American wickedness.

Nevertheless, the unfairness made me uneasy. My father had taught us that economic inequality was unfair, yet he himself accepted it all his life and never entirely freed himself from the aristocratic habits of his upbringing. He never identified with servants and underlings (as I did) or felt their humiliation and deprivation as his own. He did what he could, from his superior position, to improve their lot, but he did not feel it wrong to live well while they could not, and presumably he considered it all right for us to live in a rich man's house in Los Angeles while condemning the means by which it existed. I wish that I had been able to discuss all this with my father; I would like to have known how he came to terms with the inequality of life; but by the time it became a problem to me, I had stopped talking to him about important things. Though I had learned from him the moral absolutes of childhood, I had to work out for myself all the compromises necessary for adult life.

There was never any teen-age rebellion in our family. Since my father had always been reasonable with us and always given us as much freedom as we could manage (if not more), there seemed nothing to rebel against. His opinions on all subjects, so rational, so sound, so well expressed, were impossible to disagree with. All that seemed necessary was to go ahead and act on them in our own independent lives. But that is not growing up. We needed to test his ideals against our own experience and to modify them, where they didn't work, in order ultimately to arrive at ideals of our own. His counsel in this necessary process would have been invaluable, but we did not avail ourselves of it, for fear it would overwhelm our fragile independence.

One morning when I came down to breakfast my father asked me about a movie I had been to the night before with friends.

"Oh, don't ask me before breakfast," I said, feeling

cross because my diet didn't allow me a proper meal. Feeling also, instinctively, a need to defend myself against his knowledge of me.

He was very hurt. We didn't usually treat him that way; there were more polite methods of evasion. I knew I should not have done it. . . . He said nothing, I said nothing; we finished our breakfasts and went off to our classes, he to teach and I to learn. Later in the day Peter took me aside to tell me how much I had hurt his feelings and that I should apologize. So I did, but it healed nothing. How can you communicate with someone who has to use another person to tell you you have offended him? I am sure I was unapproachable, walled round with a six-foot fence of resentment masked with a fixed expression of surliness. It was easier to ask Peter to talk to me, since I had not yet completed my fortifications against her. It was easier, but less useful if he really wanted to approach me. If only we had not been so shy!

Since the war had made it necessary for John and me to stay in America, arrangements had to be made for our education there. John, who was nearly eighteen, went straight to UCLA without difficulty. I was only fifteen and had to go to high school. Everybody told us the public schools were academically hopeless, really out of the question, and so, on the recommendation of friends, I was sent to a private school for girls, which was supposed to be on a higher intellectual level. I attended this young ladies' establishment, in which the girls wore uniforms and asked permission for everything they did, in terror every day, being entirely ignorant of what was expected in the way of obedience and good manners. Lunch was an ordeal, for I could not understand the intricacies of American silverware manipulation and, to make matters worse, I was put at the French table, where all the good manners had to be done in French. The classes, on the other hand, were a farce. I

remember coming home one day and saying with contempt: "You know, their history book has big print and
pictures in it!"

After a month or so of misery, I was mercifully
allowed to withdraw from the school and study at home
instead, ending my school education at the age of fifteen.
I never graduated from high school and I missed much
that I should have learned, for in college I studied only
such subjects as seemed easy or interesting.

I stayed at home and studied under my father's direction, reading Plutarch's *Lives* in English and Heine on
Napoleon in German. He had me read most of the morning, then report to him on my reading, translating some of
the German and asking questions about parts I could not
understand. I enjoyed the reading very much, as both Plutarch and Heine are excellent storytellers, but I hated talking about it. I was so desperately afraid of seeming ignorant or stupid that I hardly ventured to say anything at all,
preferring to keep to myself all that I didn't know or didn't
understand.

Besides the handicap of my pride, there was the awful
obstacle of my hunger. The second half of the morning was
spent with an eye on the clock and a mind on the cavernous,
growling emptiness of my stomach, in which I knew the
tiny lunch of bouillon, lettuce and execrable cottage cheese
would be totally lost. Some days, I sat all morning in that
small library, like a great ugly lump of self-pity, looking
with angry despair at the unsympathetic back of my father
at his desk. Nobody, I thought, could really understand
my miseries and, what was worse, nobody even tried, nobody even noticed. Awkward and overweight and humiliat-
ingly blind without my glasses, I despaired of attracting
sympathy.

In addition to perennial hunger, I suffered from the
interminable eye exercises that were supposed to restore

my sight to normal. We had visited Aldous Huxley, in his dark house buried in bougainvillea, and he had told us about the exercise method that had preserved for him the little sight he had left; perhaps it had even improved it. So Peter took me off to the good ladies who administered these exercises, and I embarked on a struggle with my reluctant sense of vision. I lost. There were moments when I could see perfectly clearly, as well as any normal person; it seemed that perseverance and determination should be able to expand those moments into minutes and then into hours and even days. But it didn't happen so. They remained moments only, they even became fewer, and the sweetness of the eye ladies began to grate on my nerves. Like the diet, the eye exercises intended for my benefit became merely a burden imposed on me by others.

I did have one valid reason for grief: I was dismally lonely, and homesick for the bosom friend I had left behind at Dartington. Timmy, who was a very gentle girl, quiet and shy and blinder than I was, had befriended me on my very first day, when I was lonely and afraid, and from then on, for five years, we had gone everywhere together, with our arms around each other's waists. Now I was friendless again, totally cut off from her and worried about what might happen.

In one of her rare letters to me in America, Timmy included a picture of herself, a dim and obscure snapshot. I sat and gazed at the blotchy thing, in heaven for the moment.

"Look!" I said, showing it to Peter.

"Yes, it's very nice, but what is it?"

"Why, it's Timmy!"

"Oh . . ."

Though I was alone in my unhappiness, I was not the only unhappy one. We were all unhappy in Los Angeles, and we all *meant* to help each other, but what we understood by helping was not to complain about our personal troubles to others, whose griefs were as great or greater. Noble and self-sacrificing in conception perhaps, but dismally unsuccessful in practice. Since none of us felt free to express our grief, none of us was open to offers of sympathy from others. We lived alone, stoically bearing our burdens and refusing to inflict them on each other. "A trouble shared is a trouble halved" should have been hung up in every room of our house.

Peter was lonely in Los Angeles too, preoccupied with running a strange house in a strange place in the midst of her own anxiety about the war, and this made her more irritable than I remembered her, fussy about the housework and easily offended if we didn't leap to help her. She was always a perfectionist in domestic matters and quite unable to let things go when she could get no help, even though she hated doing the work herself. In our house in Los Angeles, standards were maintained at the expense of considerable tension for all of us, since her energy had to be replenished by frequent and perceptive praise. I still believed, however, that when Peter and my father were alone together, away from the tensions of the household, they would have the joy of each other's presence, for better or worse, to have and to hold, from this day forward. . . .

One afternoon my father invited John and me to go for a walk with him. Walking in suburban Westwood was so dull that we had almost given up our family walks, so the invitation came as a surprise. His manner was curious too and we wondered what was up. After a while, as we walked up a hill beside a feathery hedge, he said: "Peter has decided to leave us."

I was stunned. She was still my closest confidante, my most reliable admirer, my father's beautiful loving wife, with whom he lived such a gracious life. How could she leave? What had been going on?

"Oh, hm . . ." said John.

"Would you like me to ask her to stay?" I managed to get out, struggling with my embarrassment.

"Well, I don't think it would do much good"—leaving the distinct impression that he would be quite relieved if she did go.

Nothing happened. After a few days he told us, awkwardly, that she had changed her mind. My world had turned on its axis, and I saw everything from a new angle. I began remembering small scenes and tensions right back to Telegraph House. So it had not been an idyll after all, that elegant life I had so much enjoyed? More like a charade. The elegant life continued, in Los Angeles, in Pennsylvania, at home again in England after the war, but it was a gilded cage of obligations to gratitude. It grew increasingly difficult to be sufficiently appreciative, the opportunities for inadvertent ingratitude multiplied like a mine field about our feet, till we feared to say or do anything she did not command, lest we unwittingly offend and set off an explosion.

Poor Peter! Where could she have gone if she had left? A foreigner, aggressively English, not trained to anything, cut off from home by the war. Marriage to my father had been more difficult and less rewarding than she had hoped, and now that she could find no way out of it she trapped us all with her in her impossible situation.

Despite everything, we still found much to enjoy: we ate well; we had amiable conversations at meals; we went to movies together and laughed in the wrong places; we went to the beach, to the mountains, to Grauman's Chinese Theater to see the footprints of the stars. Peter and my father both had a zest for life, a capacity for enjoyment and a curiosity about the world, which made them exciting companions. Though the world might be falling in ruins, we would still see the sights, still read stimulating books and discuss them, still laugh and make jokes and mock the folly of mankind. The surface smiled and sparkled in

Los Angeles as in Wales, but the depths were darker and more turbulent, and sometimes they broke the surface with eddies of cold passion. I found it difficult to stay afloat.

My brother John does not now communicate with me in any way I can readily understand, and I do not know how he thinks and feels inside his gentle, comical, grotesque exterior. But I think I can imagine. Over and over, in describing the varied scenes of my family life, I find myself writing "it seemed . . . but. . . ." It always seemed normal, cheerful, sensible, even optimistic, but that was only *seeming*. It *felt* unhappy, angry, dangerous; life itself was threatening and usually sad. Which was right? Could one believe both without being torn apart? John could not. I solved it by allocating the good to my father and the failure and despair to myself.

Sometimes I think I should have written this book in parallel columns, the bright side and the dark side. Integration of the two seems to me impossible, for they did not acknowledge each other's existence. I believe that good and evil are essential to one another, that neither of them can exist alone and that there is envy, fear, anger, resentment, in every human heart, no matter how well brought up. My father did not believe this. Though these ugly things existed in our hearts, their existence was always denied in our family relations and they were left to fester like hidden wounds.

Of course my father had a public life in Los Angeles too, though I paid little attention to it. He was a professor of philosophy at UCLA, carrying on his work as impeccably as always, despite his many cares. Wherever he taught, my father made it his practice to get to know the keener students personally, inviting them home for tea and talk or for an evening of philosophy. Peter was an admirable hostess to such groups; she enjoyed the opportunity to impress people with her beauty and charm them with her interest—especially the young men—and her pleasure spread over the whole evening. Sometimes I felt she tried too hard to outshine my father, but I dare say if I had been his wife instead of his daughter I would have grown tired of being always in the shadows. It was of no consequence in any case, for he was the one they came to see, and he was always charming to visitors, entertaining them with his best funny stories and making sure they felt at home. Even when he was over ninety and might have felt he could leave such things to others, he remained a perfect host.

While my father was at UCLA, he was offered a position for the following year at CCNY—the City College of New York—which he accepted with some relief, as he found UCLA in many ways uncongenial. Unfortunately for him, some of the more narrowly devout Catholics of New York City decided he was not a fit person to instruct the young, because of his views on sex. A vast protest was organized, a court case was brought against the New York Board of Higher Education, the technical hiring agent, and my father found himself out of a job almost before he knew what was happening. The court ruled that he could not be a party to the suit, which concerned only the Board of Higher Education. Consequently, since the board was only too happy to accept the court's decision and be rid of a controversial character, he was left without any possibility of appeal.

It was a *cause célèbre* for academic freedom. Indignation ran high, letters to the editor were written all over the country, professors trembled and were silent, recognizing the power of bigoted ignorance to deny them a living. Liberals took up the cause and were generous with their words in his defense, which they were sure would prevail.

We sat in our house in Los Angeles reading reports in

the papers, hearing the news on the radio, receiving letters from New York three and four days after the event. It was not the first time my father had run into a storm on account of his opinions, especially in America, where the forces of obscurantism are less discreet than in England, though perhaps no more powerful. But it was the worst, because it left him destitute. When Trinity College dumped him, in the First World War, he was bitterly hurt, but he still had money to live on. In 1940, he was unable to get money out of England, unable to go home, responsible for the support of a family—and nobody wanted him to write, lecture or teach, because he was now too "controversial." We lived with anxiety and frustration and desperate uncertainty, until Dr. Albert Barnes came to our rescue.

Dr. Barnes had made a fortune out of manufacturing a patent medicine called Argyrol, which can prevent the blindness caused in babies by gonorrhea in the mother if it is put into their eyes at birth. With his money, he had built an outstanding collection of modern French paintings, which was housed in a gallery near Philadelphia and used for the instruction of selected private students. It was a *private* collection; though his wealth had enabled him to acquire many extremely famous paintings, he felt no obligation to share them, and it was extremely difficult for anyone to get permission to view Dr. Barnes's collection. He now invited my father to come and lecture on philosophy in these incongruous surroundings, thus saving us from the long, quiet death of starvation.

Having been delivered by Dr. Barnes from penury, we rented a house for the summer of 1940 on Fallen Leaf Lake, high in the Sierra above Lake Tahoe. It was like the mountain meadows above Yosemite, but lovelier. We lived in a little wooden house among pine trees, whose powerful summer scent reminded me of that hot hotel in Yosemite, though Fallen Leaf was cooler and the aroma of the pines more intoxicating than oppressive. A boat came with the house, and John and I used it to explore the lake or to row across to the store on the other side, far closer by water than by road. We walked up peaks to see views; we swam in icy lakes and sat under frosty waterfalls; we walked through mountain meadows with long green grass and delicate flowers, and the largest mosquitoes in the world. The weather was always sunny and warm enough for swimming, but never too hot for walking.

To this paradise came Dr. Barnes, by plane and hired car, to negotiate the details of my father's employment. He brought with him a little dog, which was the apple of his eye. It understood only French and had to be provided with some particular and curious food. Memory suggests that it was spinach, but perhaps I am confusing the animal with Popeye. We knew how crucial Dr. Barnes's visit was and how easily he was offended, and we understood in a moment that he was a man who lived by the adage "Love me, love my dog." Though the dog was less than lovable, we survived without catastrophe, and my father signed with Dr. Barnes a five-year contract to lecture on the history of philosophy at the Barnes Foundation, beginning in February 1941.* The five-year contract was my father's idea; he had been warned that Barnes was as fickle and quarrelsome as he was generous and that it would be wise to get a firm commitment while he was still benevolently disposed toward us. Events proved the wisdom of this advice.

The California chapter of our lives ended when my father and Peter, Conrad and Conrad's governess went east to Harvard, leaving John and me to continue at UCLA

---

* During the fall semester he was to give the William James lectures at Harvard, an agreement made before the uproar at CCNY and honored by Harvard with politely concealed reluctance.

for a year on our own, until they had a settled home for us to come to.

John lived for that year in a shabby co-operative house for men, a place for students who could not live at home and could not afford or did not like fraternity life. Most of them seemed to be poor intellectuals from out of state, getting a good education cheap, and John made some strange but comfortable friends among them.

I lived in a sorority house, where I remained hopelessly out of place despite all my efforts to adapt. I was sixteen; I still liked to go to bed at nine-thirty and, in spite of all my liberal theories, I was totally innocent, even prudish. I could not begin to understand the sophisticated sex life of my roommates, which was all carried on behind the back of regulations designed to prevent it—such rules as always leaving the door of the "date room" open when you were in there with a man. It was my first experience of the gap between official morality and common practice; up to then, I had imagined ordinary people *lived* by the conventions my parents held up to scorn.

John had been left the car, which he had learned to drive, and once in a while we would go off to the beach together, or to the mountains or some place we had not seen before. Sometimes he invited me to supper at his place, sometimes we met on the campus, sometimes we didn't see each other for a few weeks. I never invited him to the sorority, feeling quite certain that it would be a miserable experience on both sides.

Peter and my father took an apartment in the Commander Hotel in Cambridge, a tall brick building on the edge of the Common, where they enjoyed a sophisticated academic social life, while my father delivered his lectures to a crowded hall of students. They wrote us pleasant letters, we wrote to them about our studies and our trips, and there was peace in the family again.

My father was to begin at the Barnes Foundation in

February, which meant trips down to Pennsylvania to look at houses, an occupation Peter enjoyed, sending us pictures and writing amusing letters about the agents she met and the houses they showed her. At length she found one she said was charming, and she set to work with her usual energy and extravagance to create another gracious house. She made it sound so delightful that I could hardly wait to arrive at Little Datchet Farm and be with Peter again. By then I had forgotten the difficulties.

In June, when John and I were finished at UCLA, we set out to drive across the continent with three of his friends who came from the East. We were nineteen and seventeen respectively and still strangers to much of America, yet my father took it for granted that we could cross the continent alone, without any admonitions to be careful. After we had seen the Grand Canyon and some of the other colorful sights of the West, we settled down and drove and drove and drove, through endless hot countryside, with the hot wind blowing in our faces, existing in a torpor from Coke machine to Coke machine. I suppose it was an educational experience, yet I remember nothing but the blazing heat, the gas stations and the motels, until we reached the green farmlands of Pennsylvania. We got to them late in the day and debated whether to push on or to stay one more night in one more motel. Tired of traveling and short of money, we decided to keep on until we arrived at Little Datchet Farm. We had not committed ourselves to arriving on any particular day, because we did not know how long the trip would take us. So now, feeling very mature and responsible, we sent off a telegram to let them know we were coming. "Five of us arrive small hours," said the telegram, and on we went, swelling with pride at our own thoughtfulness.

The five of us turned in to the drive of Little Datchet Farm between one and two in the morning. The last part of the trip, over narrow, unmarked country roads, had been difficult in the dark, and we were relieved that it was over. The entrance to the driveway was overhung with pink rambler roses, which flashed for a moment in the headlights, and beyond them, at the end of the drive, lay the house, long and low and gray and partially creeper covered, with white-framed windows staring out at us. Inside, as I had expected, it was beautifully furnished, in a mixture of discreet modern and Pennsylvania antique, making me feel happily that I had come home to the kind of house I liked and the people with whom I felt comfortable.

We slept long and sound and woke in the morning to a good breakfast and a fine scolding. It appeared that our mature and responsible telegram had not been quite as grown up as we thought. If we had telephoned instead, they would have told us that there was not room for three extra people in the house and that we should stay one more night along the way. We had been thoughtless and inconsiderate and were made to feel duly ashamed of ourselves. John's friends, with whom we had spent a comfortable ten days on the road, now seemed gauche and uncivilized; they felt ill at ease in our home and were glad to be taken to the station, to continue their journey to New York by train.

Pennsylvania

When I saw the beauty of our new home and garden, and the familiar green peacefulness of the the surrounding farmland, I was sure that we could be happy there, taking it for granted that family relations would be amiable and that all we needed for happiness was a pleasant environment. Of course we had no friends in Pennsylvania at first, but that was nothing new to John and me, who had not had friends at home since we went away to Dartington. We expected vacations to be family affairs.

What was new for me, that summer, was the final completion of the wall that had been progressively cutting me off from the family. John had withdrawn himself from all of us as long ago as Kidlington, and the feeling of closeness I still had with him was mainly illusion. I had never had any real tie to Conrad, who was thirteen years younger and the object of my resentment, as a rival for Peter's affection. I could have tried to make friends with his governess, who was only a few years older than I was, but I was too shy. I had shut out my father the year before in Los Angeles, feeling myself unable any longer to bear the burden of trying to win his approval. I felt as he had felt about Ottoline: "The real trouble between you and me has always been that you gave me a sense of failure. . . . To be really happy with you, not only momentarily, I should have to lose that sense of failure. . . . When I have felt that through caring for you and feeling unsuccessful I have lost energy, it has produced a sort of instinctive resentment."

Only Peter was left, who had been my anchor in an unstable world ever since she came into our lives ten years before. I wanted her to be serene and confident, a woman without problems of her own, who could give me the support I needed in the difficult business of growing up in a foreign country in wartime. But she was adrift herself, confused and depressed by the problems of her personal life and much more in need of help than able to give it. She hoped I would give her sympathy, if nothing more, but I resentfully withdrew my confidence from her, and each of us was left alone with her unhappiness.

The hot, oppressive Pennsylvania summer became a long ordeal of disappointed expectations and concealed hurt feelings. It was a relief when it came to an end at last, and John and I departed for Harvard and Radcliffe, where we were to continue our education.

I loved Radcliffe from the very first day. We arrived in Cambridge in late September, leaving the humid greenness of Little Datchet for an air like wine and trees already hinting at the flame of fall. Energy came flooding back; one could go all day in that stimulating environment, where everything was new and wonderful. I sat in the library and dreamed of reading all its books, or walked along Massachusetts Avenue planning to buy a book in every one of the many bookstores I passed. At meals, people spoke of ideas and theories they were discovering in courses taught by professors who seemed high priests of knowledge, not tired hacks repeating old lecture notes.

Even the buildings, a large assortment of undistinguished academic styles, seemed soaked in learning, as ancient churches are steeped in devotion.

In those days, Harvard and Radcliffe were completely separate, and the girls had all their classes at Radcliffe, taught by professors who first lectured at Harvard, then walked across the Common to repeat the same lecture for a handful of girls in a small classroom. Radcliffe was a tolerated female dependent of Harvard, and its students were sheltered young ladies. We had little contact with Harvard men and little opportunity to meet them, outside the few official get-togethers at the beginning of the year. If you did not catch a man then, who would take you out at weekends and perhaps introduce you to some friends, you might be condemned to a whole semester of empty Saturday nights in the dorm. People like me, who were shy and unglamorous and bad at dancing, had little hope of success.

I must have been a startling person to meet. Nobody had ever shown me how to play female in the American way or even hinted that it might be politic to disguise my learning and my brains, which I regarded as my principal asset. I knew nothing of the art of flirtation, and my acquaintance with necking and petting and "how far do you go?" was still purely theoretical. My view of sex was a muddled mixture of enlightened idealism and observation of the activities of my sorority mates at UCLA. Once in a while I consulted Peter, but her advice was based on her own experience as a glamorous undergraduate at Oxford and it was not helpful. I never discussed my social life with my father, who seemed to me remote from all the trivial problems of dating in an American college, though I did still turn to him for help with more important decisions. Once I asked him whether I should sleep with an amiable young man of my acquaintance.

"Do you love him?"

"No, not really."

"Then I shouldn't. It's best to save that for someone you love and not treat it lightly."

I went to Radcliffe in September 1941. One Sunday in December, as I was sitting in my room listening to the New York Philharmonic, the real world intruded again upon my private life. "We interrupt this program to bring you the following news bulletin: the Japanese have attacked Pearl Harbor." More war. It was like August 1939 all over again, but this time I could not shut it out, because things began to change within my ivory tower.

John decided to "accelerate." The men of his class, 1943, knowing they had little chance of staying on till graduation, increased their course loads and went to summer school, in the hope of cramming through to a B.A. before they went off to war. This was called "accelerating." John graduated in January instead of June and went home to join the British navy, leaving us to worry as we read about submarines in the Atlantic. Although I had not seen much of him at Harvard, I missed him dreadfully when he was gone, especially when I had to go home without him.

The summer of 1942 had not been pleasant. John was at Harvard and I was imprisoned at Little Datchet, without the gumption to invent any kind of escape. The war brought domestic problems too: food rationing and the final, definitive disappearance of any kind of household help, which left us at the mercy of Peter's housekeeping perfectionism. "My mother used to insist on dusting every chair rung every day," she would say, feeling she was being much more tolerant and had let down standards as far as they could go. But we still spent a large part of every day on different kinds of household tasks. Gas rationing was another dreary aspect of the war, for we were miles out in the country, unable to escape from home by visiting or driving about to see the sights. We were trapped together for the summer, locked in with the heat and the dust and the prolific fruit trees, whose products must not be allowed to go to waste.

Once during the summer I did manage to escape, but not without awkwardness. I was invited by a Radcliffe friend to visit her family in their summer home on Nantucket for a week of swimming and sailing and friendly conversation. John was invited too, for as long as he could spare from his work at Harvard. He wrote and told me he was going, and asked me to tell our parents, since he hadn't time to write (and perhaps didn't want to very much). Unfortunately, the letter arrived in the midst of a storm about something, and I decided to wait until later to tell the news. "Later" never came. There was always some obstacle, and the longer I put off telling, the harder I felt it would be to explain why I had not already done so. I woke in the morning wondering how to tell them; I stewed all day looking for an opportunity; I went to bed at night ashamed because I had not succeeded in communicating this trifling piece of news. In the end, I went off to Nantucket without telling them, hoping they would not find out. Of course they did, for John mentioned it in a later letter, and then the fat was in the fire.

Why hadn't I told them? Why had I been so deceitful? Did I feel it necessary to conceal John's social life for fear they would disapprove, as they had disapproved of some of mine? Even my father was upset, for he hated underhandedness. I was called into the library and asked to explain myself to them. It was quite hopeless to try and make them understand. I simply accepted their interpretation of "deceitfulness," said I was sorry and cried with relief at having it out in the open.

Summer at Little Datchet grew progressively worse

as Peter grew more desperate. Though she must have been far lonelier than I was, her increasing irascibility made her so unapproachable that we could not help her. My father lived with her like a martyr, pretending to an affection he no longer felt, constantly attempting to appease her indignation. When nothing else worked, she would fall desperately ill and need caring for with jello and rice water until she recovered. Then, in her weakness, she would be weepy and apologetic, and we would try to be kind and reassuring, for she was truly pathetic. But when she was well again, she drove herself and the rest of us to that perfection of housekeeping which left her exhausted and us resentful—and then accused us of not appreciating all she did for us.

I used to feel that my father was to blame for her fury. Like Hitler, she expanded her demands as long as she met no opposition—and, like Chamberlain, he continued to appease her. Peter had been very young when my father first took up with her, and she must have been flattered by the stop-at-nothing passion of a famous man she greatly admired. (Like my mother before her.) But she had found marriage to the great man something of a disappointment. His passion cooled and was replaced by kindly courtesy and a show of affection thinly unsatisfying to a romantic young woman. She exacted from him the trappings of affection and he paid them to her like a tribute, imagining that she was deceived. I am sure she was not. She was still young and beautiful and did not relish being put on the shelf as stepmother, mother, housewife, beyond the need for passion.

"It is very difficult," my father told me once, "pretending to an emotion you don't feel all the time. Even when I am half asleep I have to show affection. I cannot relax for a moment."

He thought I would sympathize, but I was shocked. Was this the honesty he had taught me? Was it kindness?

Was it the right treatment for an unhappy, frustrated wife? Wasn't he only trying to pacify her for the sake of a quiet life?

I blamed my father for years for "putting up with Peter," feeling that he should have been able to do something about it. Perhaps not in America during the war, where she would have been a stranger and alone, but afterward, back at home in England, surely he could have left her, since it seemed impossible to change her? Having seen the damage done to John and me by divorce, however, he was anxious not to harm Conrad in the same way, and so he stayed. Trying to learn by his mistakes, he only succeeded, all too humanly, in making different ones instead. Conrad lived for years in a house whose atmosphere I could barely endure for brief visits, though I was almost grown up.

But for me there was always Radcliffe, just as there had always been Dartington, a fortunate escape from tension, but so much more than that. At Radcliffe I found at last a world outside my home to which I could imagine myself belonging. Though there were many difficulties involved in learning the rules and manners of this new society, I thought it would be worth the attempt, for here were people with whom I might be friends. I also found at Radcliffe, in my studies of German literature, authors who gave exact and eloquent expression to my pessimistic intuitions about life. With an exhilarating sense of liberation, I plunged into an orgy of gloomy intellectual decadence.

One day I sat in the library talking to a handsome young man who was a fellow student in one of my German classes.

"Don't you believe in any kind of God?" he asked, knowing who my father was.

"No," I said, "I don't. It doesn't seem to me necessary."

"Then what is the point of living?"

"Well, I've been born now. I have little choice. Might as well go ahead and make the best of it."

"That seems so bleak. How can you bear it?"

"Does it? Maybe. It's just the way life is, the way the world happens to have developed. Not much use wishing it were otherwise."

My godless world looked as desolate to him as a lifeless world would to me, but I was used to its impersonal freedom, never having known any other. At the same time, I was well aware that my existential despair was mere self-indulgence and that, God or no God, I would have to return someday to the humdrum world of doing good, helping individuals and mankind to the full extent of my rational benevolence, as I had been taught. Pessimism was no excuse for inaction. Nevertheless, it was pleasant to know that intelligent men had thought as I did.

At the end of my junior year, I decided to "accelerate," like John, and go to summer school. We were all getting restless for home, and money was short, for Dr. Barnes had broken his contract, as expected, leaving my father in financial difficulty again. He thought that in England he might be able to earn a living doing propaganda for the government, being for once in agreement with its policies. He wanted to go home to England, too, before Conrad was old enough for school, not wanting him exposed to the chauvinism of American schools. He had no job to keep him in America, John was already gone, and I was nearly ready to leave—why should he stay away from home any longer?

By going to summer school, I could save my father some money, be ready to return to England at the same time as the rest of the family and spare myself the misery of another Pennsylvania summer. I could not in fact have spent that summer at home even if I had wanted to, for we no longer had the big house, which my father had had to rent in order to make ends meet. He and Peter and Conrad were living in the servants' cottage across the road from Little Datchet, all miserably cramped together. They barely managed to squeeze me into a corner of the living room for the few weeks between semesters.

I hadn't been home long before one of the worst catastrophes of my life occurred. I was climbing a big tree in front of the house, with Conrad, while my father sat on the porch with a book. Peter was out shopping.

"Look at me!" Conrad said.

I moved out along the branch to see him better—*crack!* It broke, and I found myself flying toward the ground below. I think I was stunned for a moment.

"Oh, Kate! My darling Kate!" my father cried, leaping from his chair and rushing down the steps.

I heard the anguish in his voice, and the love. "I mustn't worry him," I thought, and got up carefully. My back hurt like fury, but I could move all my limbs, so I thought it was nothing serious.

"I seem to be all right," I said.

"Are you sure? Oh, thank goodness! Are you quite sure? Oh, what a terrible fall."

"Well, my back hurts. I think I'll go in and have a bath. Maybe it will help—anyway, I'm all muddy."

So that was that. I didn't plan to tell Peter, knowing she would chalk it up to my stupidity, but by suppertime the pain was too bad to conceal.

"Why didn't you tell me?" she asked. "You might have made it much worse. Now lie down and don't get up till the doctor comes."

The upshot of the doctor's visit was a painful thirty-mile ambulance ride to Bryn Mawr hospital. At the hospital, I was X-rayed and the damage discovered: two cracked vertabrae, three months in a cast followed by three in a brace. I lay on the hospital bed in the hall, en route from the X-ray department, listening from waist level as the doctor spoke to Peter and my father. Quietly I began to weep.

"She is not crying from pain, but because of the trouble she has caused," Peter explained to the doctor.

I wished she had not felt obliged to say that.

Since I had fallen into a patch of poison ivy, the doctors had to wait for the rash to subside before they could put the cast on, and I spent a couple of weeks flat on my back, in considerable pain, eating and drinking through a straw and itching at inaccessible extremities. When at last the poison ivy was cleared up, the doctors wrapped me in an immense plaster bathing suit and allowed me to go home.

The friends I had visited on Nantucket lived in Bryn Mawr, though they always spent the summer on the island. Generously they lent us their house for the summer, knowing that gas rationing would prevent frequent visits from Little Datchet to the hospital and that once I got out we would need more space than we had in the cottage. It was a pleasant, well-provided home, and we filled it with the discord of our lives. I sometimes wondered if the walls did not reflect back our bitterness into the lives of our friends after they returned.

Peter's temper had become unbearable, and there was no knowing what would set it off. She and my father were worried about money, longing for England and sick of each other's company. I was humiliated by my dependence on Peter, profoundly depressed and bored stiff by my enforced idleness. Conrad, alone with the three of us, was often querulous and difficult.

Yet it was in that summer that I found the courage to ask my father if he thought it was all right for a woman to be merely a wife and mother. We were sitting alone together in a small back porch, he reading a book and I thinking about what I should do after college. Most of the girls I knew were planning to get married—it seemed such a simple solution, so easily fulfilled. Could it be enough? Besides, I was in love. Was it possible for me to dodge the high destiny for which I had been raised?

"Do you think," I asked, very tentatively, "that it might be all right for a woman just to get married and have children and not have a career?"

It was for his sake—or so I thought—that I had struggled against that ambition all my life, so it was a hard question to ask.

"Why, yes," he said, looking at me in surprise. "Of course it's all right. Why?"

"I just wondered . . . I thought it might not be enough. . . . I mean, any fool can have children—it's a bit like being a cow. I thought maybe people like me should do something more, do something about the world."

"That depends. Any woman can have babies, or almost any woman, but not every woman can raise responsible human beings. I think if you did that you would be making a contribution to human happiness. And you would probably find time to do other things too, if you wanted to. But there's no need for a woman to have a career outside marriage if she doesn't want to. That's not the important thing."

I felt I had been given a parental blessing.

The endless summer came to an end at last, and I went back to Radcliffe for my senior year, wearing a harness that took the strain off my back while the bones finished healing. It was delightful to be able to wear clothes again, after a whole summer of housecoats wrapped around my thick plaster shape. And it was heaven to get away from home, back to an environment where I now felt thoroughly at ease. I had friends, I enjoyed my work, I began to be successful in modest ways and I did my best to put the complicated misery of home out of my mind.

In May of 1944, my father, Peter and Conrad returned

to England, leaving me to graduate from Radcliffe and follow them in June. I did not attend my graduation—there
seemed no point, with nobody to watch, and I grudged the
money required for cap and gown. I felt suddenly detached
from the college scene; my mind was with my love, awaiting overseas duty at Fort Dix, New Jersey, and my whole
preoccupation was how to see him again before I departed
for England.

It was wartime and sailings were secret; I was sent a
small piece of paper in a recycled envelope telling me date
and time of embarkation and warning me to inform no
one. Being young and selfish and indiscreet, I sent a telegram to Fort Dix: "Meet me in New York, June so-and-
so." He, being equally young and foolish and indiscreet,
went AWOL, and we spent one of those passionate wartime nights edged with despair in a quiet New York hotel.
In the grey morning, I went off with my suitcase, and he
returned to Fort Dix to talk himself out of trouble. We
approximated our lives to the movies we saw, feeling, saying and doing what the stars did when the hero went off to
war. But the anguish and the apprehension were real; we
did not know if we would ever meet again.

As the S.S. *Rangitiki* plowed slowly through the Atlantic at the tail of the convoy, America faded into the background. Radcliffe was finished and I was coming home.
When we got close enough to see the coast, to smell the
distant fragrance of bracken and heather, my heart over-
flowed with joy. I stood on the deck repeating to myself
with emotion the poem I had so often heard my father
declaim with ridicule.

> *Breathes there the man, with soul so dead,*
> *Who never to himself hath said,*
>   *This is my own, my native land!*
> *Whose heart hath ne'er within him burn'd*

As *home his footsteps he hath turn'd,*
　From wandering on a foreign strand?
If such there breathe, go, mark him well;
For him no minstrel raptures swell;
High though his titles, proud his name,
Boundless his wealth as wish can claim,—
Despite those titles, power, and pelf,
The wretch, concentred all in self,
Living, shall forfeit fair renown,
And, doubly dying, shall go down
To the vile dust, from whence he sprung,
Unwept, unhonour'd, and unsung.

Home Again

I had been in America five years, during which I had cut myself off from my mother almost entirely, thinking about her as little as possible and reading her affectionate letters with impatience. Now that I was home, the time had come to repair the breach. I went down to Cornwall, where she was spending her summer holiday, intending to establish a mature and friendly relationship with her. Almost before I knew what was happening, I found myself sucked into a new dependency, transformed in spite of myself into another of her hangers-on. It all happened so naturally: she had a big house in London, with room for me to live in it; she was working for the Ministry of Information and found it easy to get me a job down the hall from her; she knew all about the complicated routine of living in wartime England, while I knew nothing. I succumbed and moved into the house in Cricklewood, joining John, who was learning Japanese for the navy at the School of Oriental and African Studies of London University, my stepfather, Pat, who had some sort of government job, a couple of student lodgers, and my sister and brother Harriet and Roddy, when they were home from school. My mother shopped and cooked and coped for all of us, as well as managing a full-time, responsible job, and we allowed her to do it, because that is the kind of person she is.

When my father had arrived in England, a month or so before me, he had been invited back to Trinity for five years, to his great satisfaction, and had been given very pleasant rooms in the college. No provision was made, however, for Peter and Conrad, who were condemned to exist in lodgings, until it became clear that my father would finally win his lengthy suit against Dr. Barnes and be able' to afford a house. As soon as he could, my father bought a house outside Cambridge, which Peter furnished with her usual impeccable taste, and they invited John and me for a visit. We were met at the station by my father, who carried us off for a tour of Cambridge, which I had never seen before, showing us with pleasure and pride all the great old colleges and his own delightful rooms. Then, with some apprehension, we took a bus out to the house to face the uncertainty of Peter.

At the very end of our time in America, when my father was living in Princeton, relations had become so difficult that I had finally refused to go home any more. He used to visit me at Radcliffe when he had lecture engagements in New England, and we would sit together in restaurants making awkward conversation. We hoped, however, that now Peter was comfortably established in her own country again, it might perhaps be possible to maintain a more civilized relationship. Though John and I were on the alert for emotional booby traps, all seemed to go well at first, and we began to think we might have outgrown the storms. Then came the explosion. I had not been back in England long enough to know that people went visiting with little packets of butter and sugar and tea, and with ration books too, if they were staying long.

John never noticed things like that. So there we were for the weekend, empty-handed, as thoughtless as ever, sponging off them and making life impossibly difficult. We bowed our heads before the storm, apologized for our lack of consideration and departed as soon as possible, promising ourselves not to return.

I was not happy in London. I had arrived there at the end of the buzz-bomb raids, in time to spend a few anxious nights on a metal bunk in a subway station, but not in time to feel myself a part of the heroic resistance to Hitler. All I felt was shame at having escaped so much, along with even greater shame at my inability to take in stride the discomforts the others had already endured for so long. I shrank into a solitary cell of depression, which was sufficiently obvious to worry my father when I reluctantly visited him again in Cambridge. He suggested that I should see a psychiatrist and made an appointment for me with a man in Guy's Hospital.

Guy's Hospital was in a part of London remote from my office and my home, so far away that I was afraid I would never find it. I set out by subway and by bus, worrying all the way that I would get on the wrong train, get off at the wrong station, miss the bus, miss the right stop, arrive abominably late. When I got to the hospital I still had to negotiate a warren of gloomy corridors before I reached the heart of the labyrinth, the office of the doctor himself. He proved to be tall and cold, with pale hair and pale blue eyes behind glasses, a very unforthcoming person. I was too afraid to say much. Though I knew little about psychiatry and was not at all sure what to expect, I was quite sure that I didn't want to tell him *anything* about my secret, shameful self. I went to see him several times, making the long trip to the hospital, but I never trusted him enough to tell him what I really felt about anything. I didn't even realize the necessity of talking freely before he could help me. In the end, he discontinued the visits, and I sank back into my lonely apathy. It was a depressing experience.

When the war ended, the Ministry of Information was reorganized and I found myself out of a job. I had no idea how to find another, nor much notion of what I wanted to do, other than help in the rehabilitation of Germany, which I could find no way of doing. In my uncertainty, I applied to Radcliffe as a graduate student and was delighted to find that they wanted me enough to make it financially possible for me to return. And so, a little over a year after I had come home, I was off again across the Atlantic.

Though I have regretted that decision many times since, at the time it seemed necessary for self-preservation. Perhaps it was. I felt absolutely incapable of coping with the emotional strains of my two homes, yet unable to emancipate myself from either while remaining in the same country with them. I sailed away from Bristol with a sigh of relief, arrived at Radcliffe a few weeks after the beginning of term and settled down to being a graduate student.

It was quite different from undergraduate life. All of a sudden I had no supervision at all, being left to manage my own lodging, my own food, my own finances and my own program, entirely as I chose. Since many of my Harvard friends were returning from the army to finish up their degrees under the GI Bill, I soon had a pleasant informal social life. I persuaded my sister to come over to America to college too, feeling that it would be good to get her away from home and to help her adjust to more normal ways of living. I was sure I could be all the mother she needed, for I was grown up now and running my own life in a perfectly intelligent way—though at the same time I was eagerly looking around for a man who would marry me and relieve me of the burden of my independence.

I had decided to go on with the study of German, as

the safest course, and I had committed myself to getting a Ph.D. I did venture to take a few of the English courses I had been afraid to attempt as an undergraduate, only to find that they could not be counted toward a degree in German. The further I advanced in my studies, the narrower grew the field, until I felt I was being forced into a small dark tunnel with nothing in it but Old High German verbs and textual variations. This was not what I meant by education, nor was it *life*. *Life*, to me, meant love and sex and marriage and children. What was I doing in this dusty dead end? The girls I had known at Radcliffe were all getting married; few seemed to be contemplating any other career, and if they were working it was only "until . . ." After the years of war and separation, many of us felt impelled to reassert the values of permanence and union and the creation of life. I myself was possessed by a romantic ideal of mutual relationship: the man to earn money and fix things and grow a garden; the woman to cook and clean and mend and care for the children; the two together as complementary as pieces of a jigsaw puzzle. Intending to renounce the public career I thought my parents expected of me and to show them instead the beauty of a happy home, I sought diligently for a man who would help me realize my vision.

I was lucky enough to find one, a quiet and kind young man, with a dry wit that reminded me of my father. Unlike many of his ex-soldier friends, he seemed willing to settle down and accept domestic responsibility. In later years, he reproached me, whenever we quarreled, for marrying him to "set up housekeeping" and to have a father for *my* children. Though I denied it bitterly, swearing I had married for love, he was right. Nevertheless, I would not have married just anybody simply to provide myself with a home. I believed, following my parents, that love alone was not a sufficient reason for marriage, which was necessary only for the protection of children. Until there were children, unofficial and unentangling relationships were better, even between those who were profoundly in love. Charlie was the first man I had met whom I loved and respected enough to contemplate spending the rest of my life with him in the co-operative enterprise of raising children. I considered my attitude a compliment to him, but he didn't see it that way. Now that the marriage is over, I can see more clearly the disadvantages of my point of view: in my mania for motherhood, I neglected Charlie and restricted my own life unduly. As a child-raising enterprise, however, both of us would agree that the marriage was a success.

The summer after I got married, I took my husband home to England to meet my family. Having always wanted to spend my honeymoon at Carn Voel, I hoped to be able to persuade my mother to let us go down there on our own for a little while before the rest of the family came. Though I was twenty-four years old and six months married, she was not at all sure I would be able to manage the house without her, but at last she agreed to let me try, and we took off in the train for Penzance alone. I took Charlie to all the beaches, dragged him on long cliff walks and insisted on showing him everything, unable to believe that he would not at once love Cornwall with a passion to match my own. We had a lovely time until I mentioned in a postcard that we could not use the boiler for hot water, because it smoked so much. This brought my mother down almost at once, with a chimney sweep's long brush with which she most efficiently cleaned the chimney. After that, we had hot water, but the honeymoon was over.

From Cornwall we went to Wales to visit my father and Peter, who were living in a small house up in the mountains. They invited us to come and stay at the neighboring inn, since there was not room in the house.

I went with some trepidation, knowing Peter, but since we were not staying in the house, we were not too much of a burden on her and she was pleasantly gracious to us. I was relieved too to find that my father liked Charlie and they got on well together. Peter paid a visit to London while we were there and asked me to take charge of domestic matters in her absence. Unlike my mother, she assumed me capable, though her standards were so exacting that I feared what she would say on her return.

During her absence, we had one glorious day, an endless stretch of dazzling sunshine, as rare in Wales as diamonds, and we all decided to go to the beach—my father, Conrad, Conrad's tutor, Charlie and I. There we stayed all day, swimming, building castles and playing cricket. Next day found us sunburned as red as lobsters and miserably sore. My father's feet, which were unused to such exposure, began to swell painfully, and we had to call the doctor, the same old Dr. Morris who had cared for us as children at Deudraeth Castle. He told me to soak the feet in normal saline solution and looked at me with scorn when I asked him what it was.

Then Peter telephoned from London. "Is everything all right?"

"Oh yes, everything's fine."

"Conrad behaving himself?"

"Yes, very well."

"Is your father all right?"

"Yes, of course."

"Well, can I speak to him?"

"Well . . . you see . . . he's upstairs in bed."

"Is he ill? What's wrong?"

"Oh no, he's not ill. It's nothing serious. He just sunburned his feet. You see, we went to Black Rock Sands all day."

"How *could* you be so silly? I suppose you are all burned to a crisp."

"Well, yes, we are rather . . ."

"How *silly* you all are!"

We also paid a brief visit to John and his wife, Susan, and their three little girls, in their tiny, crowded house in Richmond. While I had been enjoying my happy graduate-student life, John had finished learning Japanese and had been sent by the navy to work in Washington. There he had met Susan, a daughter of Vachel Lindsay, a girl of nineteen, who already had a child and was in process of getting a divorce. She was small and rather plain, but as exciting as a smoldering volcano. Rather abruptly, John had married her, adopted her child and taken them to live with him in his grubby little Washington apartment. Almost at once they had another daughter.

When John was at last released from the navy, he returned home to England with Susan and the two little girls, and only too soon they had yet another daughter. John became a civil servant, with a job he didn't much like in some government planning office. Susan, though she was restless under the burden of three young children, was managing reasonably well, and they seemed cheerful to-gether, in spite of the cramped conditions of their lives.

When, at the end of a long summer of visiting and sight-seeing, our plane took off at last for America and I looked down on London shrinking to a toy, then the patch-work fields sweeping past beneath us, too soon followed by the coast and the ocean, I cried, realizing for the first time how foolish I had been to marry a foreigner. I should have drawn other lessons from that summer too, but I did not want to see them: my husband was not a family man, and he went along reluctantly with many of my plans, out of kindness, politeness or pure love. I simply was not aware that I was pushing him around. If anyone had told me so, I would have been horrified.

Conversion

Back in Cambridge in the fall, my husband and I returned to the preoccupations of graduate study in our separate fields. I was struggling with problems of research for my dissertation and the very different ones of teaching basic German to Radcliffe undergraduates, while he was pursuing his gift for languages along many different paths. I have never known anyone so adept at learning languages, so quick to perceive connections and to relate one language to another. He seemed set for a brilliant career in linguistics, but he was restless at Harvard, finding purely academic work as dry as I did. After a long period of uncertainty, he finally decided to give up his studies and go to work for the State Department, where he could use his abilities to what seemed more practical purposes.

We moved down to Washington in midwinter and established ourselves in one of those neat brick apartment complexes then spreading over the countryside around the city. The warmth of the climate and the easygoing friendliness of the people were pleasant after the astringent atmosphere of New England. I embarked with eagerness on the business of "homemaking," though I did pretend for a while to carry on with research for my dissertation. When I finally abandoned it, I used as excuse the fact that the topic I had chosen was hopelessly difficult and the library facilities inadequate for my research. The truth was that I found myself at last in a position to start my real life's work, the raising of a family.

When my father was in the United States on a lecture tour in 1950, he came to visit us in Washington, the first and only time he stayed in any house of mine. Having often heard him speak of the strain of a lecture tour, I was anxious to make his visit as restful and agreeable for him as possible, besides wanting to impress him with my domestic skill. But we were living in three small, ugly rooms, and our collection of secondhand furniture was still in its inception; there was no way I could make him comfortable, or even attempt to conceal the cramped improvisation of our living arrangements. Though he was as graciously polite as always, neither of us really enjoyed his awkward visit. The worst moment for me was the first, when he came wandering up the stairs and knocked on the door—and did not recognize me. I was pregnant then, and I had a different hair style, but I did not think I had changed beyond recognition in two years. It was like Miss Wogglywoo all over again, but this time it was not a joke.

My father came to America only once again, and when he visited us he stayed in a hotel, because by then we had added a baby to our crowded clutter. After that, I did not see him for a long time, for he was growing too old for long trips and we were too poor to visit England.

He and I continued to correspond, of course, but we had not much we could really share. I had immersed myself in domestic life, devoting all my energy and intelligence to becoming an expert wife and mother. I found it challenging, tedious, discouraging and exciting, but not something I could write about to my father at length. Letters were mainly reports of births and promotions, childhood sicknesses, vacation trips, some of the horrors of the McCarthy business and, occasionally, my futile dreams of persuading Charlie to move to England.

During those same years, my father suddenly became respectable, receiving the Order of Merit and the Nobel Prize and appearing frequently on the BBC—only to squander all that respectability on his increasingly strident campaign for nuclear disarmament. Not that it mattered. Respectability made him uneasy, for he was so used to considering the majority wrong that he felt comfortable only in opposition. Besides, he was right. It was far more important to arouse mankind to the dangers of its annihilation than to preserve his own position as an admired sage. Yet it was heartbreakingly difficult, for most people, including his own children, were too busy getting on with their postwar lives to pay much attention.

He gave us books to read, his own and others', and when we visited him in Wales in 1960 he talked to us at length, over the teacups, about the dangers of nuclear armaments.

"Yes, of course it would be terrible," we said. "We see that clearly. But what can *we* do about it? We have no influence. Living in Washington, we cannot even vote. We don't have time either—we're busy opposing segregation and earning a living and taking care of our children."

"Can't you see that if you do nothing about the nuclear threat there will be no people to segregate, no living to earn and no children either?"

Yes, we saw that; it was obvious. Yet we did nothing. No wonder he became increasingly shrill, finding men so foolishly indifferent to their own preservation.

More and more of his time and energy went into anti-nuclear activities. At home in the United States, I read about him in the papers, saw pictures of him speaking in Trafalgar Square, sitting in the street, on his way to prison again. He felt himself responsible for the welfare of mankind, driven by his wisdom to cry out like a prophet, hoping yet to save the children of Israel from the destruction their folly and wickedness deserved. I found myself embarrassed by his extremism and I used that as an excuse for doing nothing myself.

"What do you think of your father's activities?" people would ask me.

"He is right, of course," I would have to answer. "But I think his methods are a bit extravagant. More reasonable protests might be more effective."

After the establishment of the Committee of 100, when he began to advocate civil disobedience, my doubts increased. I was reluctant to acknowledge the ineffectiveness of rational persuasion, which he had taught me to value so highly, and hesitant to open the door to any kind of extralegal action, not being sure where it would stop. His extravagance was perhaps justified by his desperation; people simply would not listen to the calm voice of reason. Nevertheless, it did antagonize people. The war-crimes tribunal, for instance, at the time of the Vietnam War, was received with widespread skepticism, even by people like me, who were bitterly opposed to the war. We rejected his facts because of his tone of voice—but they *were* facts, as we have had to acknowledge since.

Nevertheless, I still have doubts about his methods. For the preservation of humanity, which he considered an absolute good, he was willing to sacrifice much that he had always thought valuable. "Better red than dead," he would have said, though in more elegant words. As long as there were human beings, he thought, there was hope that they might ultimately evolve a decently human form of existence. Once they had succeeded in exterminating their own species, however, there could be nothing to hope for at all. Though I would no more prefer the extinction of humanity to the victory of world communism than my father would have, I have never regarded the mere existence of humanity as good in itself, and I can contemplate without panic a world devoid of human beings. (Unwittingly, my father was responsible for this callous point of view, having taught us that mankind was no more than an accident of evolution.) My father had a far greater affection for the human race than I, and a much wider view of life; starting from the good of the human race, he worked down to individual satisfaction, whereas I do the opposite. During the years when his mind was entirely taken up with preventing nuclear destruction and mine with the tiny details of raising young children, little real communication was possible between us.

My father's personal life had changed too, putting me out of touch with his private as well as his public existence. He had finally broken off with Peter and not long afterward began his long and happy association with Edith Finch, his fourth wife. Without her, I do not know how he would have survived the personal and global anxieties that beset the last twenty years of his life. In all the newspaper pictures I saw of him, sitting, standing, marching, protesting, Edith stood in the background, in her leopard-skin coat, gentle but determined, a true supporter. I do not know Edith very well, for I was not often in England during those years, and she is as shy as I am; but all that I know I like. If I could have ordered from the Almighty a person to accompany my father to the end of his life, it would have been someone like Edith, devoted, courageous and witty.

Though Peter had gone, she had left bitterness behind: Conrad had turned against his father and refused to have anything to do with him. He was cut off from me too, far away in America and wrapped up in my own concerns. At least, I thought, he had the pleasure of one child's company, for John was living downstairs from him, with Susan and their three little girls.

Life had not been all roses for John and his family in their little house in Richmond, nor for my father, left alone in the world. They decided to take a large house in Richmond together and share it, with John's family downstairs and my father upstairs, able to mingle or separate as they chose. They hoped in this way to ease the financial burden on John and lighten the domestic load for all of them.

The arrangement lasted till Christmas of 1953, when Susan left, followed by John. Soon after, he suffered a breakdown, of which I do not know the details, for I was not there and everyone was too busy to write to me about it.

Since the three girls had been left with my father, he took over responsibility for them, sending them to school and providing them with a home in the holidays and somebody to take care of them. The school was conventional and not particularly pleasant; home was rather lonely and unexciting, for my father and Edith were not young, but at least it was stable and predictable, after the upheavals of their early years. My father felt it best for the girls to keep them away from John, and therefore he hesitated to let them visit their grandmother. My mother, on the other hand, wanted them to live with her so John could see them, feeling that he had a right to see his own daughters. She also believed my father's sedate and quiet home was bad for them.

The next time I was in England, in the summer of 1960, I had to hear the arguments of both sides, my mother's righteous indignation and my father's cold correctness. I felt the old panic of my childhood returning as I listened, the old impulse to leap up and run away, run for hours along the cliffs and never come back.

My father, in his *Autobiography*, blamed John's unhappiness on his being born after 1914 and belonging to the generation "lost by the folly and greed of the generation to which I belong." I would put it in more personal terms: it was not the whole generation that was responsible for his unhappiness, but the particular family into which he had been born. Why should he trust those people who left him alone in the dark with his fears, who plunged him into the turbulent Atlantic despite his frantic screams? Thinking of my father's childhood, however, I realize this is an oversimplification equal to his own. If anyone should have grown up neurotic, unstable, unhappy, my father should have: both parents lost by the age of four, then years and years of solitary guilt-laden existence in a house full of gloomy old people. Yet he was genuinely full of zest for life, cheerful, joyful, kindly. Nothing half so awful happened to John, yet he suffered a mental breakdown. Was it hereditary after all? Was the old family doctor right in his warning to my father to think of Uncle Willy and refrain from having children?

I do not know enough about psychology to answer this question, but about John's unhappiness, which I shared, I can speak from personal knowledge. I was the fortunate wife of a promising young civil servant with two charming children. I had everything I wanted, yet I was not happy. What was wrong with me? In those years, the constant mental dialogue I carry on with my father took the form of reading *The Conquest of Happiness*, in the hope that it might help me.

The book promised a cure for "the ordinary day-to-day unhappiness from which most people in civilized countries suffer, and which is all the more unbearable because, having no obvious external cause, it appears inescapable." It seemed made to order for me, until I discovered that he considered puritan morals the cause of such unhappiness and their rejection its cure. What help was that to me, who had been brought up without this burden? How was I to explain or excuse my steady misery? I had always believed that, although I was not yet the joyful and courageous person my father had hoped to create, I might still become so with sufficient effort and determination. If now, in spite of having everything necessary to happiness, I found myself still prey to despondency and fear, I must be a sad failure as a human being. Either that or my father was mistaken. Now that I was myself a parent, I faced an inescapable choice: either to follow my father's methods with my children, continuing to blame only myself for my inadequacies, or to hold him responsible for my failures and to follow different methods with my own.

I could not come to any decision. In desperation, I went for help to the local mental-health clinic, then once a month for a long time to see the clinic psychiatrist, the first man I ever trusted. He helped me immensely. I began to see that it was possible to feel anger and fear and even envy without being contemptible; it was conceivable that people might like me even if I stopped trying to be a model of all the virtues. He supported me through many crises and encouraged me to trust myself, but even with all his assistance I could not achieve the courage my father desired. It did not occur to me to want to achieve what I myself desired, even if I had known what it was.

Still I was not satisfied. Though psychiatry might be able to adjust me to the terms of my existence, it was powerless to make sense out of that existence. The "life" I had so looked forward to in my student days proved to be nothing but diapers and cleaning and losing my temper and feeling ashamed. Was that enough to live for? What could my father tell me about the *purpose* of living? I had learned from him to be kind and honest and reliable and to work for the good of mankind. Now I found that I couldn't do it, and I wasn't sure I wanted to. What *was* "the good of mankind" anyway, and why did it always seem to involve self-sacrifice? I asked some of his other books what he thought.

I read *Sceptical Essays* and *Unpopular Essays, In Praise of Idleness* and *Marriage and Morals*, but they all offered the same solutions: reason, progress, unselfishness, a wide historical perspective, expansiveness, generosity, enlightened self-interest. I had heard it all my life, and it filled me with despair.

In the last volume of his *Autobiography*, written toward the end of his life, my father wrote: "We feel that the man who brings widespread happiness at the expense of misery to himself is a better man than the man who brings unhappiness to others and happiness to himself. I do not know of any rational ground for this view, or, perhaps, for the somewhat more rational view that whatever the majority desires is preferable to what the minority desires. These are truly ethical problems, but I do not know of any way in which they can be solved except by politics or war. All that I can find to say on this subject is that an ethical opinion can only be defended by an ethical axiom, but, if the axiom is not accepted, there is no way of reaching a rational conclusion." He went on to speak of the "impossibility of reconciling ethical feelings with ethical doctrines" and acknowledged that in the depths of his mind "this dark frustration brooded constantly."

Reading that, I felt justified at last in my inarticulate dissatisfaction with his plausible arguments, which had never quite convinced me; they had not convinced him either.

I discovered also from his *Autobiography* that he had

not always been the rational optimist he seemed to me. He had had to struggle to keep despair at bay, and the optimistic visions of his popular books had not come easily to him; they were products of the will, maintained by determined effort against the sense of desolation that was always lying in wait for him. In moments of grief or weariness, it could overcome his ordinary hopefulness, and from the mountaintops of his vision of heaven he would plunge to the depths of hell.

In Grandmother Russell's religion, the only form of Christianity my father knew well, the life of this world was no more than a gloomy testing ground for future bliss. All hope, all joy were centered on the life after death and were to be achieved only by unceasing warfare against evil in oneself and others. My father threw this morbid belief out the window, but he was never able to obliterate the emotional pattern with which it had stamped him. All the yearnings of his powerful nature were directed to the future, to a golden age to come, if not in heaven, then on earth. All his life, he felt the old necessity to devote his best efforts to achieving future goals, at no matter what cost to himself, for the coming happiness of mankind meant more to him than his present pleasure. More than that, it was the *purpose* of his present actions.

He taught us to feel the same way. Our personal desires were to be considered less important than the good of the human race, our talents and energies devoted to improving the lot of mankind. We accepted this lifelong obligation despite the fact that, even as children, when we wrote those plays at Beacon Hill, we did not believe in the possibility of Utopia.

In his many anti-Christian writings, my father attacked over and over again the cowardice of religious people who could not face life without the comfort of their irrational beliefs. He recommended instead "the stark joy" to be found in "the unflinching perception of our true place in the world," the same proud passion I had offered my Harvard friend in our discussion in the library. Christians were mocked for imagining that man is important in the vast scheme of the universe, even the high point of all creation—and yet my father thought man and his preservation the most important thing in the world, and he lived in hopes of a better life to come. He was by temperament a profoundly religious man, the sort of passionate moralist who would have been a saint in a more believing age.

I believe myself that his whole life was a search for God, or, for those who prefer less personal terms, for absolute certainty. Indeed, he had first taken up philosophy in the hope of finding proof of the existence of God, whose childish reality had vanished before the probing questions of his adolescent mind. He needed certainty, he loved clarity with a passion, and he could not bear any kind of muddled thinking. "Either/or" was much more congenial to him than "both/and" (my favorite); "it is" was better than "it may be"; "the truth is" was preferable to "perhaps."

I could ask him a question as a child, a question about almost anything, and get a good, clear answer that began with "it's quite simple." Often it did not seem simple to me, and that made me feel stupid. Many of the complications I sensed, however, were real; not all questions are "quite simple," and his answers were not as unambiguous as he intended.

"Do we have free will?" He said "no," writing philosophically; but he acted "yes" and wrote "yes" when his moral passions were engaged.

"Is there progress in the world?" He might say "no" and make fun of the sillier versions of it, but he acted "yes" and based his life on the hope of it.

On a more trivial level, I might say, as a small child: "I don't want to! Why should I?"

To which a conventional parent would reply: "Because you must."

But why?"

"Because I say so . . . your father says so . . . God says so. . . ."

My father would reply: "Because more people will be happy if you do than if you don't."

"So what? I don't care about other people."

"You should."

"But why?"

"Because more people will be happy if you do than if you don't."

We felt the heavy pressure of his rectitude and obeyed, but the reason was not convincing—neither to us nor to him.

Somewhere at the back of my father's mind, at the bottom of his heart, in the depths of his soul, there was an empty space that had once been filled by God, and he never found anything else to put in it. He wrote of it in letters during the First World War, and once he said that human affection was to him "at bottom an attempt to escape from the vain search for God." After the war, finding his life more satisfying, he stopped talking that way; nostalgia for religion was quite absent from our home. Nevertheless, I picked up the yearning from him, together with his ghostlike feeling of not belonging, of having no home in this world.

One Sunday, in Washington, a friend asked me to go with her to the local Unitarian church and help her run the coffee hour after the service. Almost my only experience of church had been many years before, as a child in Wales, when my father had decided that, as part of our education, John and I should at least know what a church service was like. The parson was a Welshman, naturally, with the up-and-down Welsh way of speaking, and he took as his text "I know that my redeemer liveth." In the course of his sermon, he repeated the text many times, coming back to it again and again to examine it from a different angle—an excellent sermon technique, except for his Welsh voice. "I know that my redeemer liveth," he squeaked over and over, until John and I were reduced to helpless, shameful giggles. The experience dissuaded us from further church attendance quite as effectively as my father had intended; I had been to church perhaps three times since, each time to fulfill a social obligation. Though I went along now to oblige my friend, I was not expecting much.

Nevertheless, I found myself strangely impressed. There was something that appealed to me, some vague promise of an answer to my problems. I went home and thought about it for a long time. Finally, summoning all my courage, I said: "Charlie, would you think me very stupid if I went to church once in a while?"

After a lifetime of scoffing, it was hard to say.

The next Sunday, he went off to the Episcopal church, leaving me at home with two fretful children sniveling with bad colds. After that, we got together and began going to church more or less regularly, and as we went on going, Sunday by Sunday, I listened attentively to the hymns, the prayer book, the words of the Bible, even the sermons.

As I listened, I began to think that what I heard made sense out of everything. Nothing that was said contradicted what I had learned from my father, and I was not offered a faith full of the absurdities he delighted in ridiculing. The enlightened Episcopalians I heard had apparently listened to the criticisms of people like my father and dropped the follies of the past. I could not have believed in my great-grandmother's God any more than my father could, but here I met one who was quite credible. And I found it easier to believe in a universe created by an eternal God than in one that had "just happened."

Before I started going to church, I had been running about the world, like Christian in *Pilgrim's Progress*, looking for a way to escape the burden of my sin, and neither my father nor psychiatry had been able to help me.

"It's irrational and unscientific to feel as you do," he told me. "You have nothing to feel guilty about."

"Nobody is perfect," psychiatry told me. "Don't expect so much of yourself."

But I remained "weary of earth and laden with my sin," just like my father in his youth. His jettisoning of his own imprisoning religion was no help to me, for so much of it had remained with him unaware. Once, on a trip to Greece made late in life, he visited a small Byzantine church and found to his astonishment that he felt more at home there than in the Parthenon. "I realized then," he wrote, "that the Christian outlook had a firmer hold upon me than I had imagined. The hold was not upon my beliefs, but upon my feelings. It seemed to me that where the Greeks differed from the modern world it was chiefly through the absence of a sense of sin, and I realized with some astonishment that I, myself, am powerfully affected by this sense in my feelings though not in my beliefs." I could have told him that about himself, but he would not have believed me.

The religion my parents had grown up with was a dry morality without grace, a series of impossible demands that left them defeated and depressed. They escaped from it joyfully into a free life that affirmed their own goodness and expected their children's. And yet they passed on to us the same impossible demands from which they had suffered—no, not exactly the same, for they allowed us to masturbate and talk about sex—but they still expected perfect honesty and kindness and all the rest, without showing us how it was to be done. Consequently, we in our turn were loaded down with inescapable and, to us, inexplicable guilt. The doctrine of original sin gave to me, when I came to understand it, the same sense of intoxicating liberation my father had received from sexual emancipation. It was *normal* for me to be bad, and I need not feel ashamed.

For me, the belief in forgiveness and grace was like sunshine after long days of rain. No matter what I did, no matter how low I fell, God would be there to forgive, to pick me up and set me on my feet again. Though I could not earn his love, neither could I lose it. It was absolute, not conditional. My earthly father loved me only when I was good (or so I believed). I was not good; therefore he did not love me. But God did and does and always will.

I realized that there were weaknesses in the Christian argument. I acknowledged that it was difficult to reconcile omnipotence with suffering and with free will; but they were equally difficult to reconcile with "Science." Perhaps Christianity was not a logically elegant and watertight demonstration of irrefutable reality, but what choice did I have? It saved my sanity, if not my life.

All that my father said about the absurdity of Christianity and the wickedness of the church remained true. I could not deny it. But it was only a part of the whole. He seized on the follies, which are many, and labeled them official religion, while claiming that Christians have never taken seriously the good parts of Christ's teaching. But he never dealt with it seriously either. When he wanted to attack religion, he sought out its most egregious errors and held them up to ridicule, while avoiding serious discussion of the basic message I found so liberating. I found no message in his books but failure and despair (for me): men *can* be . . . men *should* be . . . men rightly brought up *will* be . . . the world *might* be. . . . But what about *is*? The world was not what he hoped it might be, and neither was I, nor could I believe that men would ever become the intelligent paragons of his imagination.

As I went deeper and deeper into religion, however, I found it ever more satisfying. I wished I could convince my father that it *added* to all I had learned from him and took very little away. I did not find it a denial of life, a brier patch of restrictions, but a joyful affirmation. "I am come that they might have life and have it more abundantly," said Jesus. All that I lost was my anxiety—and the option, perhaps, of sleeping with many men, which I had no desire to exercise. I was already so bound by the exacting moral code my father had taught me that I saw no new restrictions in Christianity, merely the possibility of living with those I already had.

I would have liked to convince my father that I had found what he had been looking for, the ineffable something he had longed for all his life. I would have liked to persuade him that the search for God does not have to be vain. But it was hopeless. He had known too many blind Christians, bleak moralists who sucked the joy from life and persecuted their opponents; he would never have been able to see the truth they were hiding. He should have been a saint; he had the passion, the intemperate longing for truth and justice, the yearning for a world of peace and love. Perhaps he was a saint, even without the faith. God's gadfly, sent to challenge the smugness of the churches with a righteousness greater than their own.

I could not have persuaded him, could not even talk to him about religion. All I could do was trust him to God's care, knowing that God loved him more than I did and would do what was best for him.

The Last Years

My father had looked forward for years to having children; he loved all three of us and enjoyed our company through all the years of our youth. Like most parents, he hoped that when we were grown up he would be able to enjoy our adult company and be proud of our adult achievements. Instead, he found himself cut off from all three of us: from John by his breakdown, from Conrad by his (temporary) hostility and from me by my religion. He continued to love us all, and I continued to love him; he and I exchanged affectionate letters, but without real communication. There was not much neutral ground on which to exchange pleasantries. If God existed at all, I thought, He must be vastly more important than *anything* else—after all, He was the creator—and He must therefore be my first consideration in *everything* I did. Like a person in love, I thought of Him constantly and could not imagine ever taking Him for granted, living comfortably with the notion of His existence while carrying on my own life in my own way. Like most people in love, I was a bit of a bore. To my father, who not only did not share but actively disapproved of my enthusiasm, I must have been tiresome in the extreme.

Luckily for my personal life, my husband did share the enthusiasm. He was as fascinated by God as I was, and we began to feel that a God so important should lay claim to the whole of our lives, though we were not quite sure how to offer them to Him. After long reflection, my husband decided he should leave the State Department and go into the ministry, even though that meant three years of unpaid study leading to a notoriously ill-paid career. It seemed to both of us the right thing to do.

I wrote with some trepidation to my father and mother to tell them of our decision, which was not likely to please them. Since, however, they had always believed that people should act on their convictions, regardless of the consequences, they now took a deep breath and said, in their different ways: "Well, if that is what you believe, of course you must act on it."

We did not know what we would live on during the years of study, but we were not worried, being young enough and devout enough to commit ourselves cheerfully to God's care, in which we had absolute confidence. The care that God provided included considerable financial assistance from my father, which prompted me to write to him that I thought God must be amused by the irony of the situation. He wrote back to say that he didn't know about God, but certainly the officials of the Bank of England, whose permission he needed to send us money, had been very much amused.

While theological college was an exciting intellectual adventure for my husband, for me it meant primarily more work and less money. Domestic detail imprisoned me, and I found myself resenting his pleasure in a most unchristian fashion. I tried to be noble and offer it all up to the love of God, but without much success. Feeling sorry for myself and longing for a change, I looked backward for a solution, as I always did, and thought of going home to England to see my parents and introduce them to their grandchildren. My father's last visit to the United States had been in 1951, when our first child was a young baby. Now I wanted him to know and admire all three of our progeny, and them to meet and love their grandfather, as well as their grandmother and all their English uncles and aunts and cousins.

My mother had managed to get over once to visit us, but in rather comical and unsatisfactory circumstances. She had come as a delegate to the United Nations for the Women's International Democratic Federation, an organization considered so appallingly subversive by the American authorities that they could hardly bear to allow its delegates into the country. Though of course they could not deny them access to the United Nations, they determined to keep them in quarantine and gave them special restricted visas, which confined the delegates to central Manhattan. My mother could not go below Fourteenth Street or above 125th Street, and she could stay only as long as the meeting lasted. As a visit to us in Washington was thus out of the question, we went to visit her in her hotel, with David, who was three, and Annie, who was a little over a year old.

Staying in a hotel with two such small children was something of an ordeal. David rode up and down in the elevator in his pajamas, and Annie climbed on the table in the dining room, smearing Cream of Wheat all over the spotless tablecloth.

"You know, Kate," said my mother, seeing my face, "you should never be embarrassed by things your children do that are not really bad. They are only young, not naughty."

By the time his father was in seminary, David had no more than a dim memory of "green Grandma" (in her green overcoat), who had given him a marvelous book about a taxi, while Annie remembered nothing and Jonathan had never even seen her. It was high time for a visit.

We went first to visit my father and Edith in Wales. They were living in Plas Penrhyn, a house close to Portmeirion, in North Wales, now filled with my father's familiar treasures. He sat in his armchair by the fire, with his feet on the same old lovely rug, surrounded by his ivories and his Chinese paintings, his books and all the remembered friends of my childhood, just as he had always done. The whole room, even the whole house, seemed an extension of my father's character. Small and old, a bit deaf and a trifle frail, he sat there in his slippers, pouring tea by the fire, like any old man. But out from him radiated his spirit: his wit, his learning, his love of beauty and passion for truth, reflected on the walls around him and spreading out from the house over all the country and all the world. I felt his greatness more then, as we sat quietly over tea in Plas Penrhyn, than at any other time.

He was a perfect grandfather. He gave the children wonderful presents and grandfatherly bits of money, and talked to them intelligently about things that interested them, so that they soon ceased to be shy. And he told them all his best stories, the ones I had loved most as a child. I have a vivid memory of him sitting by the fire, ancient and wrinkled and strange, perhaps even a little frightening, telling them about Mysie with the golden leg.

"There was once an heiress," he began, "a very rich young woman, who lost a leg in an accident. She was far too grand for a mere wooden leg, so they got her one made of gold. In due course, she married a handsome villain who cared only for her money. After he had spent all she had, he murdered her at night and ran off with the golden leg. Soon after, she came haunting him by night, as ghastly as ghosts usually are."

Here he would lean forward in his chair, open his eyes wide and declaim, in a sepulchral Scots voice:

"Mysie, Mysie, whaur's yer beautiful blue e'en?"

"Mould'ring in the grave."

"Mysie, Mysie, whaur's yer beautiful rosy cheeks?"
"Mould'ring in the grave."
"Mysie, Mysie, whaur's yer beautiful gowden hair?"
"Mould'ring in the grave."
"Mysie, Mysie, whaur's yer beautiful gowden leg?"
"You have it, you thief!"—shouting suddenly, to make small listeners jump out of their skins.

At my special request, he also sang them the song about old Abraham, comic in itself, and irresistible in his deep, solemn, inaccurate voice.

Old Abraham is dead and gone,
We ne'er shall see him more.
He used to have an old greatcoat
Which buttoned up before.
He also had another coat
Which was of a different kind:
Instead of buttoning up before,
It buttoned down behind.

Our two boys used to watch him smoking his pipe, going through the ritual of knocking it out, cleaning it with the three-legged man, refilling it, lighting it, puffing deeply to get it going, and they were filled with ambition to copy him. When we went shopping in Portmadoc they bought pipes with their pocket money, and Grandpa gave them some of his tobacco to smoke. They felt honored and important and tremendously grown up. David carried it off with distinction, but Jonathan was only five; he disappeared suddenly into the bathroom, to emerge empty, pale green and shaking.

"I'm sure it wasn't the pipe!" he gasped.

My father always treated children with respect, as equals, and offered them grown-up pleasures, for which most people would have considered them too young. Far from depraving the young, this treatment flattered them into behaving with the responsibility he expected of them. When David visited him later, as a teen-ager, his grandfather offered him Scotch, without any suggestion that he should limit his intake. David was charmed and would not have thought of disgracing himself by getting drunk.

Sometimes we all walked in the garden after tea, enjoying the velvet lawn, the opulently exquisite flowers and the view across the estuary to the mountains. One day Jonathan took a picture of his grandfather, a charming view from five-year-old eye level up to the pipe and the bush of white hair against the sky. It reminded me of the way my father had looked to me long ago in Cornwall.

The visit to my father in Wales was a fabulous holiday, the grandest and pleasantest I have ever known. We did not stay in the house, which had not room for all of us, but in Portmeirion Hotel, at my father's expense. He rented a car for us too, so that we could explore the countryside; we had no work at all, magnificent weather and every day a tea party with my father and Edith. It was so overwhelmingly luxurious that I was almost embarrassed; it did not suit my conception of our relationship to be treated with such lavish generosity by my father.

Although I accepted it all and even looked for more, imagining him richer than he was, I did not believe that he *owed* his grown-up children anything, nor that I deserved the apology he offered for doing more for John's family than mine. Their need was clearly greater than ours, and I was proud of our greater independence. So proud that I barely noticed how much my father actually did for us: how he managed to get money to us in various ways, how he helped with Charlie's theological education, how he paid for our holidays. Just as, reading his letters as they came, I missed all the affection in them because I did not believe in it. I failed to notice what was before my eyes because I was always looking for more. One day recently I sat down and read all his letters to me, and I was over-whelmed by the love and concern expressed in them, the many kinds of help they spoke of. The feeling of my life, no doubt reflected in this book, has been that he cheated me of my rightful due of affection; yet, as far as I can observe the facts, this feeling was mistaken. If there was a failure, it was of communication, not of affection.

Of course there was a failure of communication. Even from that blissful holiday I came away feeling dissatisfied, though mostly with myself. I wanted to tell him about God, to share with him the happy certainty I had discovered. And I wanted to justify myself. I did not want him to think I had swallowed a lot of nonsense and prejudice for the sake of a specious peace of mind.

But we sat at tea around the fire, the four of us, making conversation about the state of the world, and I could never break through to real talk. Too shy, too selfish, too subservient, too proud, always a follower of the tone set by others, I sat and allowed myself to be cut off from him by the small talk I had never mastered. It was only as we said good-bye that emotion broke through for a moment and I hugged him with demonstrative affection. But he was old and fragile, almost ninety; he needed to be held in tender hands, like old porcelain, and treasured for what he was. Too late for storms of emotion, too late to stand up and justify myself against him, defending my values by attacking his. Adolescent rebellion is absurd in middle age, if not cruel, and adolescent emotion is not much better. There seemed no solution but to look at each other with love as we drifted apart on our separate rafts of belief.

From Wales, we went to Cornwall to visit my mother. From quiet, expensive elegance, serenely presided over by Edith, to a shabby chaos of vibrant life. Everyone was there: Harriet and her husband, Roddy, John's girls and

John, and now five Taits. My mother cooked and coped for us all indefatigably, with varying quantities of inept help from those whose consciences reproached them for their idleness. Her generosity and her energy were fantastic.

The Tait family went off every fine day to the beaches and enjoyed every minute of it. It gave me tremendous satisfaction to share the joys and beauties of my childhood with my children; to see them climbing where I had climbed, jumping where I had jumped, sampling the dubious delights of bitter sloes and unripe blackberries. Everything was perfect except the people, with whom I experienced my usual difficulties. In the early days of my religious enthusiasm, I used sometimes to wish I could be a nun, escaping from the endless demands and problems of people and spending my time in happy contemplation of the perfection of God. Like my father, I have always found people difficult. It is easier for me, as it was for him, to feel comfortable with rocks and trees and visions of perfection.

Summer ended at last. Leave-taking was the usual mixture of sorrow at leaving the country and relief at escaping from the family, in whose presence I still felt like a cretinous dwarf.

Back in Washington, we had one more year of seminary, and then we had to discover what God wanted us to do next. As God's wholehearted servants, we were naturally ready to take ourselves, our lives and our children wherever He might want us to go, as long as it was not the suburbs, to which we felt ourselves totally unsuited.

We thought about the mission field. My husband's interest in "spreading the good news" had helped to stimulate that of his classmates, and the seminary had responded to their interest with a proposal to assist a theological college in Africa. After careful consideration, they decided to assist the theological college in Mukono, in Uganda, with money and men for as long as such help might be useful. It seemed natural that we, who had been so zealous in the cause, would be among those going, but Charlie, who had spent two days in Uganda, was convinced that he could never fit in there. What were we to do? Believing that God demanded sacrifice and that it would be a shame to let down the others, we decided to go to Uganda and do our best.

Our first and most tangible reward was the opportunity to spend a year in England in preparation for our work in Uganda. Charlie was assigned to work as curate to a vicar in Plymouth, who had himself been a missionary and knew what we would need to learn. We started our life of sacrificial devotion with another idle summer as guests of my respective parents in Cornwall and Wales. That summer has run together with the preceding one in my mind, in an indistinguishable tapestry of pleasure and pain: Portmeirion in the sun, the wild Welsh mountains, the vertiginous battlements of Harlech Castle, my father in his garden with Edith; rain and mist and long train journeys; the sun on the bay between Porthcurno and Treen Castle, heather and gorse and my mother's incomparable Sunday dinners, worshiping in the ancient granite chill of St. Levan parish church; all mixed in with inarticulate disagreement, disapproval and distress. The summers ran together in my father's mind too and appear in his *Autobiography* as one; but in fact his generosity repeated itself, as did my mother's. Both gave time and money with open hands, so that we might have a pleasant summer two years in a row.

At the end of the summer, we went to Plymouth, and by great good luck we found a house big enough for us all, a bleak old freak, full of ancient hideous furniture, moldering quietly in a row of respectable houses in a delightful part of Plymouth. This monster had two living rooms, six bedrooms, miles of back passages with larders and pantries and sculleries and such, a fireplace in every room, a huge attic full of antique treasures and no kind of central heat.

The winter was cold, with the awful numbing grey dampness peculiar to England, and all of us were busy all the time fetching in coal and carting out ashes. Even Jonathan, who was six, learned to light the kitchen boiler and was assigned to do it every morning before breakfast, so that we could eat without shivering.

"Now I know why the English drink so much tea," Charlie said, warming his hands on his cup as his father-in-law always did. "They do it to keep warm."

I remember Plymouth with affection, because our fourth child was born there, in that awful house, in a fire-warmed bedroom, at half-past three in the morning, attended by the doctor and the midwife, his father and his aunt. When it was all over, Harriet went down into the dark cold kitchen and made tea for us all, which we drank in the large bright bedroom while the baby slept his first live sleep.

From Plymouth we went to Uganda, where we spent two frustrating years, and from Uganda back to the United States, to a rich suburban parish, which proved as unsuitable for us as we had always thought it would. From there to New York for two years of mere existence, waiting for something better to turn up—at least it was so for me. I hated every minute of those urban years. Then, at last, the wreckage of our marriage washed up on the hills of northwest Connecticut, where it finally broke apart.

During those dismal years I thought often of my father, from whom I had felt unhappily distant ever since our last visit to Plas Penrhyn. I would have liked his help in my sorrow, but did not know what to ask for or how to ask. Nor did I think it proper to be still burdening him with my problems, at his age and mine, occupied as he was with the far more vital questions of peace. I wrote occasional dreary letters, which worried him, but there was nothing he could do. It was high time I took charge of my own life and made my own decisions, though I did not want to. Above all, I did not want to recognize and acknowledge the total shipwreck of my marriage, which must have been plain to all but me.

I had promised myself, when I was young, that *my* marriage would last, *my* children would have a stable, harmonious home, *I* would never tear them apart as John and I had been torn. I did not want to see that all this had already happened, even though we were still living in the same house.

Profoundly isolated in my misery, I longed for human sympathy. Slowly it dawned on me that I had created my own solitude, building with my own hands the prison walls that now surrounded me. I thought of my father, of all he had done for me, of the many times I had fended off his affection or accepted his gifts without acknowledging the love that prompted them. "He is more than ninety years old," I said to myself. "Probably I shall never see him again. I must write while there is still time and tell him how much I love him, more than anyone else in the world. I must thank him for all he has done and all he has been in my life."

So I did. I wrote, with all the "yes, buts . . ." standing round my desk and all the old complaints crowding my pen, but I fought them off. "Not this time," I told them. "You have had your day. Let me for once tell the good side, which is just as true as the bad, though you don't like to admit it. Go away. I am going to write a love letter for once in my life." It was good that I did, for indeed there was not much time left.

One morning at breakfast the phone rang. It was a friend from Wellesley. "If I can do anything, Kate, let me know."

"Do anything about what?"

"You don't know? Your father died yesterday. We heard it on the news."

"Oh . . . thank you. . . . No, I didn't know. . . . Yes, if there is anything you can do, I'll call. . . . I don't know yet what I will do. I don't see how I can go over there, and what would be the good anyway, now he's gone?"

I hung up the phone, told the family, finished up the morning chores and went out to drive to the high school where I taught, twenty-five miles from home. It was raining. White mists hid everything but the wet road ahead of me. The heavens are weeping for him, I thought, and the truth is shrouded in mist. "Sentimental idiot," I told myself, but the heavens and I went on weeping. Is he really and finally dead? Is that the end of him? Was he right, after all? God, he can't be finished, can he? A man like that doesn't just stop—you will want to see him and talk things over with him—I will want to see him again, without the hindrances that have kept us apart. Bleak rain, bleak mist, grey road, leading from unhappy home to abominable school—and now he is gone. I wept as I drove, feeling utterly abandoned. Then the stubborn optimism of my parents joined with the ragged remnants of my faith: no, this is not the end; he has arrived with God and is getting all his questions answered at last, and someday I shall be there too, with both of them.

I drove on to school and went on with life in a world without my father. I had told myself often: he is so old, so deaf, so cut off from me, it's as though he were dead already; it won't be too bad when it happens. But it was too bad, and it left me with a numb ache for a long time: now I can never tell him this, never ask him that, never straighten out old confusions—never until I am dead too, and who knows how long that will be?

It was a long time before I thought of writing about him. I will tell the world what a great father he was, I said to myself, how wise and witty and kind, how much fun we always had. They mustn't think he was always a cold and rational philosopher. So I thought, and so I began to write, but it has not come out that way. The "but"s and complaints seized my pen and forced it to record them. "He loved truth, you know," they urged. "You cannot honor him with a lying memoir. You must set down all that was wrong, all that was difficult and disappointing, and then you can say: 'He was the most fascinating man I have ever known, the only man I ever loved, the greatest man I shall ever meet, the wittiest, the gayest, the most charming. It was a privilege to know him, and I thank God he was my father.' "

Identification of Quotations Appearing in the Text

Chapter 1. The Garden of Eden

Chapter 2. Ancient History

Chapter 3. "A Generation Educated in Fearless Freedom"

Chapter 4. Beacon Hill School

Index